Managing
COLLEGIATE SPORT CLUBS

Managing

COLLEGIATE SPORT CLUBS

David O. Matthews, EdD
University of Illinois at Urbana-Champaign

Leisure Press
Champaign, Illinois

Library of Congress Cataloging-in-Publication Data

Managing collegiate sport clubs.

  Bibliography: p.
  1. College sports—United States—Organization and
administration.   2. Athletic clubs—United States—
Administration.   I. Matthews, David O., 1920-
GV351.M36 1987   796'.07'1173   86-27633
ISBN 0-88011-284-0

Developmental Editor: Sue Ingels Mauck
Copy Editor: Timothy O'Brien
Production Director: Ernie Noa
Assistant Production Director: Lezli Harris
Typesetter: Yvonne Winsor
Text Design: Keith Blomberg
Text Layout: Denise Peters
Cover Design: Jack Davis
Photos in Text: Provided by Lanie Lass, Division
              of Campus Recreation, University of Illinois at
              Urbana-Champaign
Printed by: Braun-Brumfield, Inc.

ISBN: 0-88011-284-0

Printed in the United States of America

10 9 8 7 6 5 4 3 2 1

Leisure Press
A division of Human Kinetics Publishers, Inc.
Box 5076, Champaign, IL 61820

Acknowledgments

This is the first definitive book on collegiate sport clubs. I am indebted to all of those persons, including Will Holsberry, Executive Secretary of the National Intramural-Recreational Sports Association, who gave permission for several previously published articles to be a part of this publication. Special thanks go to Art Tuveson, Loretta Capra, Sam Hirt, Larry Cooney, Dale Phelps, Sue Skola, Judy Heller, and George Haniford, who have given their time and efforts so dedicatedly to the development of sport clubs over the past 25 years.

Two former graduate students who were closely associated with me at the University of Illinois are Dr. James A. Peterson and Dr. Rainer Martens. The former, once owner of Leisure Press, encouraged the compiler of this work to gather the material and assemble it for printing. His concern about the worth of such a publication provided the continual incentive needed to see it through to completion. Rainer Martens, sport psychologist and prolific author in his own right, is the owner of Human Kinetics Publishers, Inc. His willingness to produce this book is a tribute to his zeal in seeing that the profession of campus recreation, as the main sponsor of sport clubs, finds its day in the sun. In addition, Jesse A. (Tony) Clements, Director of the Division of Campus Recreation of the University of Illinois, provided me with the time and resources to complete this book. His assistance needs to be cited, as does the cooperation provided by Dale Carruthers and Craig Stinson of that organization.

The bibliography at the end of this book was originally compiled by Art Tuveson of the University of Maryland. It was a project of the Sport Club Special Interest Section of the National Intramural-Recreational Sports Association.

It must be emphasized that the efforts of all persons engaged in the administration of sport club programs are hereby recognized as contributing immeasurably to the physical, mental, and emotional welfare of thousands upon thousands of participants in the collegiate sport clubs.

Special appreciation also goes to my wife, Dorothy.

David O. Matthews
Editor

Contents

Foreword

This unique book in the field of recreational sports has been written especially for the administrator of sport clubs. Many such administrators have contributed their thoughts to the content of this book, and their ideas have been gathered, organized, and carried to completion by Dr. David O. Matthews, who envisioned the book in the beginning, and who is a well-known and well-respected leader in the field of recreational sports.

Although sport clubs have been a part of campus life since the early 1900s, only in the last two decades have they become an integral part of the recreational sports program. Their proliferation during recent years reflects the nature of their importance to the recreational, competitive, and athletic needs of students. With this kind of rapid growth, the sport club administrator needs to be increasingly well-informed about such matters as management, legal liability, safety, fund-raising, budgeting, marketing, scheduling, and the democratic process—all in order to help student leaders develop for themselves the skills that are necessary to administrate club activities and to serve the unique needs and interests of each particular group.

This text will give the reader a wealth of information about all of these topics, and will help the sport club administrator meet the challenge of assisting the thousands of students who choose to participate in sport club programs every year.

Will M. Holsberry
Executive Secretary
National Intramural-Recreational Sports Association

Preface

The delineation of the development of the sport club movement in schools of higher education in the United States has great gaps in the recording of club organization because early written documentation on the activity of clubs is not readily available, if it exists at all. The following paragraphs briefly describe the history of sport clubs in this country.

Certain writers (Mueller & Reznik, 1979; Mull, Bayless, & Ross, 1983) report that varsity intercollegiate sports programs began in the 1850s, emanating from sport clubs in certain eastern United States, mostly Ivy League, institutions. However, there is a paucity of information about these collegiate organizations and other types of sport clubs and how they were operated. Leonard (1984, p. 27) states that "in 1732, the first non-college affiliated sport social club, the Schuykill Fishing Company, was organized in Philadelphia, and it was followed much later by the formation of a fox-hunting club in Gloucester City in 1776." Other community sport clubs were established in the ensuing years.

Other authors of intramural-recreational sports texts (Beeman, Harding, & Humphrey, 1974; Means, 1973) make the claim that it was not until the 1860s that collegiate sport clubs developed into some form of varsity organization and competed on an intercollegiate basis. However, Leonard (1984, p. 27) reports that intercollegiate sports were in their infancy in the late 1700s, and that as early as 1787 the Princeton faculty banned interclass wrestling and a prototype of football because of their brutality.

The histories of other sports would lead one to believe that college and university students in the late 1700s and early 1800s participated in the sports that they learned in their hometowns, and that they introduced these sports to their "eating clubs" at their respective educational institutions. Historical records indicate that there was competition on an interclass level at most of the eastern U.S. colleges and universities by the early 1800s.

Menke (1947), quoting from a book by Herbert Manchester called *Four Centuries of Sport in America*, states that "some species of football was played at both Harvard and Yale as far back as the 1820s, but it was more of a means to haze the freshmen" (p. 411). Because there was no organized intercollegiate sport at that time and because a number of the students lived in housing units called clubs, one can assume that in these clubs we have the origins of collegiate sport clubs in the United States.

Baseball in its developmental stages on the college level was played in an informal way at Harvard, and probably at Yale and Princeton, as early as 1820, and perhaps even before that. Official records indicate that Oliver Wendell Holmes once told a reporter of a Boston newspaper that baseball was one of the sports of his college days at Harvard (Menke, p. 86). He graduated in 1829, so he must have been playing with a student club as early as 1825. Students at Harvard could have been playing a game called "rounders," which was the precursor to baseball as an organized, rule-bound sport.

Though bowling was known to have existed as early as 5200 B.C. in Egypt (Perkes, 1978), the sport had its beginnings in Germany in the Middle Ages. It is no wonder that it was introduced to America as a well-established game by the Dutch in the very early 1800s. In the story by Washington Irving, Rip Van Winkle talked about the "thunder of the ball colliding with the pins." New Haven, Connecticut (home of Yale University) saw the introduction of the game about 1835 (p. 225). It was banned because of the gambling involved. Yale University students were playing tenpins at that time.

According to Menke (p. 822), Yale adopted a certain form of rowing in 1843, and a club was formed that year. A challenge between several eating clubs took place on campus that same year. In 1845, scholars at Harvard took up oarsmanship, but contests or regattas were interclub only until 1852, when Harvard met Yale in a match (Perkes, 1978).

Lacrosse, indigenous game of the American Indians, became known to the white man by the name of baggataway, and rules were developed for play. College students played the game in the 1850s (p. 671). In 1857, students at St. Paul's Academy in New Hampshire organized sport clubs to compete against other teams in boat racing and cricket (Chamberlain, 1944).

Between the last four decades of the 1800s and the first ten years of the 1900s, student-directed programs of intramural sports evolved. Gradually the faculty assumed control of both the intramural and the intercollegiate sports programs. In almost all cases, these programs were for the male students. Little was heard of sport clubs as an integral part of the intramural program structure, even though by 1920 great progress had been made in the development of intramural programs.

The Western Conference (Big Ten) Association of Intramural Directors was established in 1922. From 1922 to 1958, there had been mention of sport clubs in the minutes of those 36 annual meetings only ten times (Van Hoff, 1970). The first record of sport club organization *on any sizable scale* was in a report given by Intramural Director M.J. Chapman of the University of Illinois, who told the audience at the 1939 meeting that "hobby and *sport clubs*, picnics and square dance groups were promoted and publicized" (p. 27). In 1941, Chapman is quoted as saying, "Corecreational sport clubs were formed through the intramural department at Illinois. The clubs ran themselves and had access to facilities on Sundays and three evenings." He went on to say, "The program appealed to many persons not otherwise engaged in intramurals" (p. 32). The University of Illinois probably promoted sport club programs more than any other of the Big Ten schools from 1939 until the report of a highly organized program at Purdue University in 1958.

In 1958, at the ninth annual conference of the National Intramural Association (NIA), George Haniford, Associate Intramural Director at Purdue University, made the first formal presentation of any length about sport clubs. The report was titled "The Role of Sports Clubs in the Modern Intramural Program" and was published in the *Proceedings of the NIA*. At that time the NIA included most of the intramural directors of the Ivy League schools, where sport clubs were purported to have had their beginnings.

Since 1958, approximately 70 articles pertaining to sport club administration and philosophy have been published in various proceedings, magazines, and journals. Other presentations that were not printed have been given at other meetings. In addition, a number of master's and doctoral theses concerning sport clubs, along with one monograph (Cleave, 1984), dealing with club administration have been written.

In 1974, a survey of 2,011 educational institutions in the United States and Canada (Juncker, Anderson, & Mueller, 1975) revealed that from 12,000 to 16,000 sport clubs existed in North America. An average of ten students per club would mean that about 120,000 to 160,000 persons in these educational institutions were engaged in organized sport activities other than intramurals and intercollegiate sports.

There is reason to believe that interest in the sport club movement has increased tremendously in recent years. Some evidence of this is reflected in the fact that in 1975 a Task Force on Sport Clubs appointed by the National Association for Sport and Physical Education (NASPE) of the American Alliance for Health, Physical Education, Recreation and Dance published a report in which it was stated that NASPE had taken the position that "sport clubs were a desirable extension of intramurals and intercollegiate sports" (Arnold, 1975).

Also, since 1977, the National Intramural-Recreational Sports Association (NIRSA) has provided time at its annual meetings for special sessions devoted to sport club administration. Speeches, along with other types of presentations, have been made a part of the annual proceedings of NIRSA.

At the present time, between 65% and 70% of the 4-year institutions of higher education in the United States and Canada sponsor some sort of sport club program. The clubs in these programs may range in number from 1 up to 45. The schools with club programs have, in most instances, designated a person to be the sport club coordinator or director, which indicates that these institutions are putting more emphasis on the importance of this part of their total campus recreation program.

For the past 40 years, the editor has promoted the establishment, growth, and development of sport clubs. His work as a director of intramural-recreational sports programs has allowed him to closely monitor the progress of many sport club programs nationwide. He foresaw the need for greater emphasis on the promotion of sport clubs when in 1970 he predicted that, ''almost all of the directors in this country will have experienced a very drastic change in the character of their programs with co-recreational sports and *sport clubs* being the major areas of interest within the total program. . . . Sport clubs will have taken the place of varsity minor sports for a certainty and in many schools will even replace football and basketball as the main focus of attention on campus sports'' (Matthews 1971).

In 1977 the first National Conference on the Administration of Sport Club Programs was held on the campus of the University of Illinois. At that summer conference, it was strongly recommended that a ''handbook'' for sport club directors be compiled and made available for those persons on college campuses who were responsible for the organization and administration of sport club programs. In fact, it was suggested that the many papers presented at the time should be the nucleus of such a book.

The need for such a ''handbook'' has increased since that time, as evidenced by the efforts of the members of NIRSA's Sport Club Committee to assemble the material for such a publication. I have been gathering articles from sport clubs and traveling to many campuses to determine what is happening in the sport club world and to produce a definitive text about sport clubs.

Present-day administrators of sport club programs are still seeking advice and information as to what the best accepted practices and procedures are for administering their club's activities. There is no doubt that a compilation of the best literature and research available on the subject of sport club administration is of immense value to campus recreation directors. This text is designed to assist those supervisors in the management of their sport club programs.

The articles included in this book represent a small portion of those available. They were the most up-to-date and most effectively presented the material critical to sport club administration and development. Space limitations made it necessary to exclude many fine articles.

The book is divided into five parts followed by several appendices and a bibliography. Part I is comprised of articles more theoretical in nature that deal with sport club administration and organization. Part II presents articles that stress student participation in the direct administration of clubs. Part III focuses on the financial operations of campus clubs, whereas part IV includes several articles dealing with risk management and legal liability. The final section, part V, compares the results of four nation-wide studies on sport club administration and organization, which span the years 1968 to 1984.

The appendices contain some valuable tools for sport clubs, including a constitution and sample policy and procedure statements. An up-to-date directory of associations and organizations in the United States and Canada whose central theme is amateur sport and sport clubs and a comprehensive bibliography provide a wealth of resources for anyone involved in existing or new sport club programs.

REFERENCES

Arnold, J. (1975). Club sports in universities and colleges. *Journal of Health, Physical Education and Recreation, 46*(8), 19-22.

Beeman, H.F., Harding, C.A., & Humphrey, J.H. (1974). *Intramural Sports: A text and study guide.* Dubuque, IA: Wm. C. Brown.

Chamberlain, E.B. (1944). *Our independent schools: The private school in American education.* New York: American Book Company.

Cleave, S.L. (1984). *Managing the sport club program: From theory to practice.* Champaign, IL: Stipes.

Juncker, D.F., Anderson, B.D., & Mueller, C.E. (1975). Sport club development: 70s community involvement. *Proceedings of the Twenty-Sixth Annual NIRSA Conference* (pp. 144-147).

Leonard, W.M. (1984). *A sociological perspective of sport* (2nd ed.). Minneapolis: Burgess.

Matthews, D.O. (1971). The next fifty years in college and university intramurals. In L.L. Neal (Ed.), *The next fifty years . . . health, physical education, recreation, dance* (pp. 45-54). Eugene, OR: University of Oregon Press.

Means, L.E. (1973). *Intramurals: Their organization and administration* (2nd ed.). Englewood Cliffs, NJ: Prentice-Hall.

Menke, F.G. (1947). *The new encyclopedia of sports.* New York: Barnes.

Mueller, C.E., & Reznik, J.W. (1979). *Intramural recreational sports: Programming and administration*. New York: Wiley.

Mull, R.F., Bayless, K.G., & Ross, C.M. (1983). *Recreational sports programming*. Palm Beach, FL: Athletic Institute.

Neal, L.L. (Ed.). (1971). *The next fifty years . . . health, physical education, recreation, dance*. Eugene: University of Oregon Press.

Perkes, D. (Ed.). (1978). *The official Associated Press sports almanac 1978*. New York: Grosset & Dunlap.

Task Force on Club Sports of the National Association for Sport and Physical Education of the American Alliance for Health, Physical Education, Recreation, and Dance. (1975). *Club Sports in Colleges and Universities*. Unpublished manuscript.

Van Hoff, J.J. (1970). *A synthesis and analysis of the minutes of the meetings of the Intercollegiate Conference of Faculty Representatives (Big Ten) Intramural Directors from 1922-1968*. Unpublished master's thesis. University of Illinois, Urbana.

PART I

Sport Club Administration
and Organization

C ollegiate sport clubs greatly influenced the development of the intramural sports movement in America. The extremely enthusiastic and sometimes rowdy response of college students in the early 1900s to the contests between sport clubs inevitably led to faculty control, as evidenced by the formation of intramural departments with appointed directors. According to physical education history books, sport clubs were also the forerunners of varsity sports programs in America. The growth of these "stepchild" varsity programs, however, soon overshadowed sport club activities. Eventually, sport club programs almost disappeared from the college scene, except where they were absorbed into intramural structures.

Sport clubs grew gradually during the first five decades of the twentieth century. As indicated in the preface of this book, the sport club movement expanded phenomenally from about 1960 up to the present. Much of this growth was due to the influence of Title IX. This federal legislation, enacted in 1972, profoundly affected physical education, intramural sports, and varsity athletic programs. Sport clubs were greatly affected by Title IX because it mandated that girls and women be given the same opportunity to participate in sport programs as boys and men.

Consequently, campus recreation directors were required to admit women to sport clubs at their institutions. Although some sport clubs had previously included women members, before the enactment of Title IX most sport clubs were primarily for men. Title IX also required varsity sports programs to establish teams for women and girls where none had existed previously. Athletic directors were faced with the immediate problem of securing funds to finance these new teams, which needed coaches, uniforms, facilities, trainers, and transportation. Athletic departments obtained additional money through various means, but they also took action to finance women's teams by decreasing the number of men's teams. In addition, departments often cut back on the quality of the programs. In many instances, teams were eliminated from the varsity program.

The effects of Title IX have become quite apparent in recent years and have been a major factor in the current resurgence of interest in sport clubs, which is unparalleled in history. Although college enrollments have increased, varsity teams for men have remained practically the same in size. In terms of the numbers of people involved, the real increase in varsity participation has been in women's programs. At most institutions a few hundred male and female team members are given the opportunity to compete with teams from other institutions, but at each school hundreds of additional students desire the same experiences. Most athletic associations face dire financial problems as they try to carry on intercollegiate competition for as many different teams and sports for men and women as the National Collegiate Athletic Association requires for the various division levels. At most colleges, football and basketball must bring in enough gate receipts to pay for the other, non-revenue-producing sports, and in many instances the income is not matching expenditures.

Because of the financial problems created by the enforcement of Title IX, many athletic departments are naturally reluctant to add other teams to the program. Consequently, the desire of many students for some type of intense athletic competition has led to the phenomenal growth of the sport club movement. Evidence of this tremendous growth is seen in recent surveys, that almost two thirds of the universities in the United States and Canada have some type of sport club program.

Although the impetus for the renewed interest in sport clubs appears to have stemmed from students who wished to compete at the intercollegiate level in sports such as soccer, rugby, hockey, and sailing, many thousands more are involved in the organization and operation of sport clubs that do not compete. These noncompetitive clubs encompass activities such as mountain climbing, canoeing, caving, horseback riding, skiing, scuba diving, and hiking.

Because intercollegiate athletic departments generally do not wish to assume responsibility for the clubs, the task of trying to aid club members in the administration of their programs has usually fallen to directors of campus recreation. The clubs had to have a "home," and most clubs turned to the intramural/recreational sports departments and to the student affairs offices for advisors and financial assistance.

At many schools, these campus recreation directors have reserved courts, fields, and pools for the traditional intramural and informal recreation programs. They have also purchased equipment and supplies for the major scheduled sport activities. It is logical, then, that sport club members have turned to campus recreation directors for facilities and equipment. In most cases, the intramural/recreational sport administrators have been very willing to relinquish some facilities and to loan out some equipment to sport clubs. In many schools, however, the lack of adequate funds for intramural sports has made it impossible for the clubs to be totally subsidized for expenses such as room, board, and travel for competitive meet trips. Likewise, certain clubs need equipment that most intramural departments cannot afford. Expensive items such as sailboats, gliders, skeet ranges, sculling shells, and horses usually must be provided by the clubs themselves.

In recent years, the number of college and university sport teams on the varsity level has declined significantly. This decline has been a result of the cutbacks necessitated by the lack of money available to athletic departments. Gate receipts have fallen considerably for most schools, and some schools have been forced to eliminate their football and basketball teams, which traditionally have been the money-makers for the entire sports program.

The number of sport clubs has increased rapidly to fill the void in sport programs caused by the demise of varsity teams. The burgeoning development of sport club programs in North America has required these clubs to be supervised by faculty members and has caused general responsibility for administrating the clubs to be placed within some administrative structure of the institution. The resulting decisions about where the clubs would best fit has caused most sport club programs to be housed in their institutions' departments of campus recreation. The most recent survey (Goldammer & Edmonston, 1984) showed that the sport club program was under the jurisdiction of the directors of recreational sports in 61 percent of the schools surveyed, with the remainder under the aegis of the student affairs office or the administrative chair of the college.

Acceptance of administrative responsibility for sport clubs by college presidents or chancellors has led to the appointment of full-time professionals to head up the club programs on campus. This, in turn, has created a pressing need for more information concerning the best methods and procedures for administration of sport club programs. Numerous articles have been written, conferences and workshops have been held, and special interest sections have met at annual meetings of the National Intramural-Recreational Sports Association to discuss adminstrative techniques for coordinating sport club programs.

This book is intended to provide the directors or supervisors of sport clubs at educational institutions with information to assist them in conducting club programs. Part I deals with sport club administration and organization. The first of five articles was written by Shirley Cleave as the introduction to her published manual on the administration of sport clubs. She presents a model based on "The Management Process in 3-D" by R. Alec Mackenzie. Mackenzie identifies five major functions of the administrator including planning, organizing, staffing, directing, and controlling, and divides each of these functions into a number of activities.

The second article, by David O. Matthews, is concerned with the organization of sport clubs in secondary and higher education institutions. The author presents a procedure that any administrator can follow in starting sport clubs. The topics covered include determining student interest, organizational meetings, club constitutions, facilities and equipment, rules and regulations governing club activites, and club evaluation. The second part of this article addresses certain philosophical questions that face a college or university sport club administrator.

The third article selected for this section, "Organization and Administration for New Sport Club Directors," was written by Sam Hirt. In this article Hirt has listed a number of suggestions that a new supervisor of sport clubs would do well to follow. The article's main topics include the present status of existing sport club departments, setting goals, and total involvement of participants, helpers, and spectators.

The fourth article, "Alternative Methods of Sport Club Administration," was written by Judy Heller and Sandy Vaughn in 1975 and was updated in 1985. Its main thesis is that every institution of higher education has different facilities, personnel, and organizational structures with different philosophies and goals and that therefore, no single formula for sport club administration is ideal for every situation.

The last article, "Negotiating for Sport Clubs' Off-Campus Play Spaces," is coauthored by Don C. Bailey and Sue A. Robinson. As the article's title suggests, many institutions do not have enough space, if any at all, for the many types of sport clubs. Therefore, sport club supervisors, members, and advisors must seek facilities off campus. This article deals very effectively with problems and solutions relating to accessing facilities for sport club activities.

REFERENCES

Goldammer, B., & Edmonston, C. (1984). Comparison of university sport club programs in the Big 8, Big 10, PAC 10, Southeastern and Southwest athletic conferences. In B.C. Vendl, D.C. Dutler, W.M. Holsberry, T.C. Jones, & M. Ross (Eds.), *Interpretative aspects of intramural recreational sports* (pp. 225-230). Corvallis, OR: National Intramural-Recreational Sports Association.

CHAPTER 1

A Theoretical Framework for the Organization and Administration of the Sport Club Program

Shirley Cleave
University of New Brunswick

To be effective, the organization and administration of any program, including a sport club program, must be based on sound administrative theory. Several models have been developed by a number of authors to explain the administrative process. The exact model that is selected to serve as a guide in the development of the program is probably not as significant as the fact that a workable model is being used. The use of a model provides a systematic method for developing the program and helps to ensure that all important functions are considered. "The Management Process in 3-D," developed by R. Alec Mackenzie, will be used as a framework for the following discussion concerning the organization and administration of the sport club program. Mackenzie identifies five major functions of the administrator: *planning, organizing, staffing, directing,* and *controlling* and divides each of these functions into a number of activities. Each of these functions will be discussed in turn (Mackenzie, 1969).

PLANNING

Mackenzie identifies the seven activities of the planning function as (1) forecasting, (2) setting objectives, (3) developing strategies, (4) programming, (5) budgeting, (6) setting procedures, and (7) developing policies.

The first step in the planning function is to *forecast*, or establish where the present course will lead. To make a reasonable forecast, the administrator must have an accurate perception of the present. The total club program, the individual clubs, and the present organizational and administrative system must be carefully evaluated. In addition, the administrator must conjecture as to the needs and interests of future students because the student population is in a constant state of flux. Student initiative and participation are essential to ensure the continuity and growth of the various sport clubs.

After establishing the current situation and considering the future, it is necessary to *set the objectives* of the program. The establishment of the objectives or purposes of the sport club program is a critical activity because it forms the foundation upon which the program is built. The purposes of the program provide the rationale for decisions governing specific policies and procedures. For example, if extramural competition is considered to be an important objective, an effort should be made to assist with travel expenses. If clubs are strictly recreational in nature, travel funds are not likely to be needed.

In addition to the general purposes of the sport club program, specific annual objectives should be set. These might include improving the accounting system or improving communications between the clubs and the sport club coordinator. Individual sport clubs should also be encouraged to establish general purposes and specific objectives.

The third step in the planning function is to *develop strategies*, or decide how and when to accomplish the stated objectives. One part of this step involves deciding which activities should be included in the sport club program.

Several definitions have been proposed for the term "sport club" or "club sport." Most of these tend to center around the concept of joining together for the purpose of participating in a particular sport. The definition adopted should include the identifying features such as "student organization," "participation in intra- and/or inter-club competition," "largely self-supporting," "provision of instruction," and so forth. The definition should also include any restrictions placed on the sport club program. For example, some institutions include only clubs whose primary focus is *gross* motor activities within the category of sport clubs.

Programming is the fourth activity in the planning function. This entails establishing the priority, sequence, and timing of the steps necessary to meet the objectives of the program. Programming must include both short-term planning (1-year period) and long-range planning (3- to 5-year period).

Budgeting, or allocating resources, is the fifth step in the planning function. One of the positive features of the sport club program during the current tight financial situation at many institutions is that clubs can raise a significant portion of their operating budgets on their own. Because sport clubs do raise a significant portion of their own money, they naturally demand—and should be given—reasonable autonomy with respect to how this money is spent. However, clubs that receive grants from the institution must recognize the responsibilities this entails. They must maintain accurate, up-to-date records and must conduct their programs according to the guidelines for such clubs established by the institution. Thus sources of funding must be considered when the policies and procedures for the sport club program are established.

Budgeting refers not only to financial resources, but also to facilities, equipment, and administrative time. Each sport club must be allocated an equitable share of all available resources.

The last two steps of the planning function are *setting procedures* (standardizing methods) and *developing policies* (making decisions on important recurring matters). Establishing policies and procedures increases the efficiency and effectiveness of the organization and helps to ensure that all clubs in the program are treated equitably. Each sport club program should prepare a comprehensive policies and procedures manual, and each club executive should have a copy of this manual.

ORGANIZING

The four activities in the organizational function are establishing a structure, delineating relationships, creating position descriptions, and establishing position qualifications.

The first step in the organizational function is the *establishment of a structure* in which the program can operate. The organizational structure used for the sport club program varies considerably from institution to institution and depends to a large extent on the organization of the institution itself. Jamerson (1969, p. 48) found 18 different administrative agencies responsible for the sport club program. In the interests of efficiency and control, one unit should be assigned responsibility for the sport club program. The intramural sports department is perhaps the most logical choice because of the sharing of facilities and equipment and the administrative expertise available.

The second step in the organizing function is to *delineate relationships*, or define liaison lines to facilitate coordination. The relationships among the individuals involved in the sport club program can be shown graphically in the organizational chart. Sport club personnel must know to whom they report and also who is reponsible to them. They must also understand the chain of command so that they know whom to consult on various matters pertaining to the sport club program. A sport club council can be a valuable tool in maintaining a relationship among the individual sport clubs and in coordinating the total sport club program.

Creation of position descriptions is the third activity in the organizing function. Position descriptions, or job descriptions, define the scope, relationships, responsibilities, and authority of the various individuals involved in the program. The constitution of each individual club should specify the responsibilities and authority of the various members of the club executive. The duties of the club's faculty/staff advisor and/or instructor must also be clearly outlined. There should be a written job description for the sport club program coordinator.

The final step in the organizing function is the *establishment of position qualifications*. Some clubs require that club executives be full-time students who have been members of the club for at least one year. This helps to ensure that the executives have some experience, and that the club is organized and administered by the students. The key qualifications for faculty/staff advisors include genuine interest, knowledge of the sport, and the ability to work well with students. The qualifications necessary for the instructor will depend to a large degree on the type of sport involved. All instructors should have some form of recognized certification. In high-risk sports such as scuba diving and sky diving, certification by the appropriate governing body is mandatory.

STAFFING

The four steps that comprise the staffing function are selection, orientation, training and development.

The staffing function begins with *selection* of qualified people for each position. The personnel involved in the sport club program can be divided into two categories: professional and volunteers. In many programs the sport club coordinator may be the only individual who has professional responsibility for the sport club program. Ideally this individual should have not only a background in physical education, sport, or recreation, but also administrative competencies and the ability to work well with students. This individual is responsible for maintaining the framework within which the program operates. The other personnel in the program include club executives, faculty/staff advisors, and instructors. The administrator will have very little control over the selection of the club executives because these individuals are usually elected by the club membership. Sport clubs are usually responsible for recruiting their own faculty/staff advisors and instructors. In some cases the selection is made in consultation with the sport club coordinator, but in most cases advisors simply volunteer their time. Some clubs hire professional instructors or coaches to look after the instructional component of their programs. If grant funds are to be used to remunerate the instructor, the sport club coordinator should be involved in the selection process.

The second stage in the staffing function is the *orientation* of new personnel. This is a critical step because the transient nature of the student population means that some new people will always be involved in the administration of club programs. Responsibility for orienting new personnel should be shared by the sport club coordinator and the outgoing club executive. The sport club coordinator should meet with the outgoing and the incoming club executives to discuss such areas as responsibilities, organizational structure, polices and procedures, current problems, and possible future directions.

Training is the third step in the staffing function. Because the success of the sport club program is largely dependent on the efforts of the club members, it is important to provide some form of training for club personnel. Workshops can be an effective tool for training club personnel. The following are some of the topics that should be discussed: leadership styles, decision making, delegation of duties, program planning, budgeting, supervision, and evaluation.

Developing personnel is helping them to improve their knowledge, attitudes, and skills is the final stage in the staffing function. Involvement in the sport club program can be an excellent learning experience for the students because they are responsible for the administration of the club program and must learn to live with the consequences of their decisions and actions. The sport club coordinator and the faculty staff advisors should be willing and able to offer advice, assistance, and encouragement as necessary, but ultimately students learn most by doing.

DIRECTING

Mackenzie identifies five activities in the directing function: delegating, motivating, coordinating, managing differences, and managing change.

Delegation involves assigning responsibilities and exact accountability for results and is frequently accomplished through job descriptions. In the sport club program, delegation can be achieved through individual club constitutions that specify the responsibilities and authorities of the club executive and other personnel such as the club advisor and instructor. Club executives must also be willing and able to delegate certain responsibilities to other club members. Effective delegation is a key to total involvement and commitment by all the sport club members.

The second step in the directing function is *motivation*. The personnel involved in the organization and administration of the sport club program are often highly self-motivated because they have a vested interest in the success of the program. The club executive must be able to motivate the club members to work for the benefit of all. The sport club coordinator or faculty/staff advisor will have to act as a motivator primarily in two situations. The first occurs when a club is encountering difficulties and has become discouraged. The second occurs when club personnel must be persuaded to follow the policies and procedures that have been established to facilitate the operation of the total sport club program. The majority of personnel involved in the program are volunteers, and there are few, if any, material incentives. Therefore, the sport club coordinator must assist the clubs to run worthwhile programs that are rewarding in themselves.

In Mackenzie's model, the third activity in the directing function is *coordination*, or relating efforts in the most effective combination. Although each club operates fairly independently, the sport club coordinator is responsible for coordinating the efforts of the individual clubs into a total sport club program. The use of a sport club council composed of a representative from each club can be a valuable tool in coordinating the program. Whether this council is an advisory committee or a decision-making group, it can serve to enhance communication within the sport club program. The sport club coordinator is also responsible for ensuring that the sport club program functions within the context of the total recreation program. Each club president must be able to coordinate the work of the executive and the other club members to ensure the smooth operation of the individual clubs.

Mackenzie's fourth step in the directing function is the *management of differences*, or the encouragement of independent thought and the resolution of conflicts. One of the characteristics of a sport club is that it is a student-initiated and student-operated group. Club members should be encouraged to think for themselves and to solve their own problems. The sport club coordinator should allow the clubs as much freedom to operate as possible, provided they function within the framework of the club constitution, the program guidelines, and university policies. However, the coordinator must be kept informed of the actions of the clubs. Some conflicts are inevitable whenever a group of people must work together. The sport club coordinator should serve as a resource person in intraclub and interclub conflicts. The sport club council, by improving communication and understanding, can often help to resolve conflicts of an interclub nature.

The final aspect of directing is *managing change*, or stimulating creativity and innovation in achieving goals. To be effective, change must be managed; it cannot be allowed to happen in an uncontrolled fashion. Change should not take place simply for the sake of change. On the other hand, one of the unique characteristics of the sport club is the rapid turnover in membership and the resulting variety of ideas and opinions. The sport club coordinator should not only encourage creativity and innovation, but should also help the club select the best alternatives from the ideas that are proposed.

CONTROLLING

The last function in Mackenzie's model is that of control, which includes establishing a reporting system, developing performance standards, measuring results, taking corrective action, and rewarding personnel.

The first step in the controlling function is to *establish a reporting system*. This involves determining what critical data are needed and how and when they will be collected. Because the sport club coordinator is ultimately responsible for the sport club program, he must be kept informed of the activities of the individual clubs. Clubs must at least submit a written activity report and financial statement. Standard forms should be provided for these reports to assist the clubs in the preparation of their reports and to ensure that all the necessary information is recorded. Clubs should submit activity and financial reports at least once a year and preferably once a term.

Controlling also entails *setting performance standards*. Performance standards should closely correspond to the purposes of the program. Some of the characteristics of a quality sport club program include (1) an optimum opportunity for all interested individuals to participate in the sport of their choice, (2) an optimum opportunity for all clubs to participate on and off campus, (3) a high level of instruction available for all from novice through advanced, and (4) improvements with respect to the quality of facilities, equipment, instruction, and so forth. Individual clubs should also establish their own performance standards. For example, a club might strive to increase its membership by 25% or to raise enough money to buy new equipment.

Measuring the results, or ascertaining the extent of deviation from the goals and standards, is the third activity in the controlling function. This evaluation should take two forms. First, there should be a continual evaluation process that monitors the ongoing activities of the clubs. Second, there should be a year-end evaluation that reviews the whole year's program in light of the performance standards.

The fourth step in the function of control involves *taking corrective action*. This requires making adjustments in plans, counseling club personnel to help them attain desired standards, and replanning and repeating the entire cycle. The sport club coordinator should meet with the sport club council and/or individual club executives throughout the year to discuss problems and make necessary adjustments. At the end of the year the personnel involved in the sport club program should meet to evaluate the past year and plan for the next.

The final step in the cycle is that of *reward*, involving both praise and discipline. The sport club coordinator should provide regular constructive feedback for both successful and unsuccessful ventures. Because most of the personnel involved in the sport club program are volunteers, remuneration is seldom given. Instead, other forms of recognition must be developed, such as appreciation banquets, appropriate gifts, publicity in local newspapers, and so forth. Unfortunately, it is sometimes necessary to discipline club executives or other members for failing to live up to their responsibilities or for behaving in an inappropriate way. The options that are available to discipline club members will vary depending upon the particular institution.

Admittedly, the operation of a good sport club program is a difficult and time-consuming task, as this monograph indicates. Though the students should be given as much freedom to operate as is practical, at no time can the sport club coordinator assume that the program will function by itself. The sport club program poses many challenges for the coordinator and other club personnel, but it also provides opportunities for satisfying and rewarding experiences for all those involved.

Acknowledgment

This chapter was originally published in *Managing the sport club program from theory to practice* (pp. 1-6) by S.L. Cleave, 1984, Champaign, IL: Stipes. Copyright 1984 by Stipes Publishing Company. Reprinted by permission.

REFERENCES

Mackenzie, R.A. (1969). The management process in 3-D. *Harvard Business Review*, **11-12**, 80-87.

Jamerson, R.E. (1969). Pros and cons of sports clubs. *Proceedings of the 72nd Annual Meeting of the National College Physical Education Association for Men*, 48.

CHAPTER 2

Sport Club Organization in Secondary and Higher Education Institutions

David O. Matthews
University of Illinois

According to physical education history books, sport clubs were the forerunners of varsity sports programs in the United States. These sport clubs also had a great influence upon the development of the intramural movement in this country. The enthusiastic response of early college students to the contests between clubs inevitably led to faculty control, as evidenced by the information of intramural departments with full-time directors.

The growth of varsity programs soon overshadowed the sport club activities, until the latter had almost disappeared from the college programs except where they were absorbed into the intramural structures. The weaknesses of the varsity programs, however, have in recent years become quite apparent and have been a factor in a rejuvenation of interest in sport clubs that is unparalleled in modern history.

SECONDARY SCHOOL SPORT CLUBS

Though the growth of sport clubs has occurred primarily on the college level, there are excellent reasons why these clubs could become popular on the secondary levels as well.

Foremost among these reasons are those related to finance. Others are tied in with the professional concern that physical educators and administrators would logically have about the physical welfare of their students. From the financial standpoint, because almost the entire cost of the club is absorbed by its members, there would be little if any additional burden placed upon the already financially strapped physical education-athletic programs. The professional concern of administrators for the physical development of their boys and girls is alleviated by the clubs, because these student organizations provide the best possible medium for the continued and concentrated participation in activities that most interest the members.

Once an intramural director decides to begin a sport club program, certain proven patterns of action may be followed. These are elaborated upon in the following paragraphs.

1. *Determine the interests of the students*. Interest sheets can be distributed to all students through any method that will assure complete coverage. On the interest sheet may be listed all of the sports that can be thought of. The list may include as many as 30 or 40 sporting activites.

Ask the students to list or number, according to their order of preference, those clubs they would like to be in. The lack of facilities should not deter the director of the sport club program from making his or her interest list as extensive as possible. The ingenuity and enthusiasm of the students can often help overcome an apparent lack of facilities.

2. *Arrange for organizational meetings*. When the sign-up sheets have been returned, a name list for each prospective club can be made up. Once the lists are compiled, arrangements can be set up for the first organizational meetings.

Each person signing up for a club should be notified of the time and place of the first meeting. Besides individual notices, posters or newspaper announcements can be used to inform the student body of the meetings. At least two such meetings should be called so that if a person misses the first, he or she can attend the second.

The meetings should be held at a time when most students are free. For secondary school students, this might be before school begins in the morning; during lunch periods, if they are long enough; or immediately after school. Evening or weekend meetings are seldom satisfactory.

The meeting could begin with the introduction of the advisor or other faculty person who is chairing the get-together. The name or type of club being organized should be given and a roll call taken of the interested persons attending.

Next, time should be taken to explain such matters as the relationship of the intramural or physical education department to the club, the possibilities for growth and development of the club, the types of equipment and facilities needed to carry on the club activity, the rules and regulations governing any club, and the probable costs of membership.

Following the introductory remarks, a general discussion should be held to enable each person to express opinions, expound ideas, or ask questions. Individuals who have participated in the sport previously should be asked to tell the group the good points as well as the drawbacks that are associated with the activity. For instance, if a scuba club is to be organized, it is good to point out the thrills of underwater diving, but the dangers of the bends and of drowning should also be emphasized.

Experienced students can be appointed to act as temporary officers until the club has been organized long enough to hold elections. An advisor to the club can be selected. After the meeting the officers and the advisor can arrange for a future session for the purpose of getting the club better or permanently organized.

3. *Have the club write a constitution*. Constitutions serve a worthwhile purpose in that they delineate the requirements for membership, the duties of the officers, and such other things as meeting times. A standard outline form can be used so that each club can more easily write a constitution.

4. *Assist in any way possible to have facilities and equipment provided for the club without going to great expense, if any at all*. If the prospective club needs gymnasium, pool, or field space to carry on its sport, consideration should be given to its needs after class, varsity team, and intramural program demands are known. The type and location of the school will definitely affect the allocation of time and space for clubs. Perhaps the club can be allowed to use the school facilities at special times during the day or week when the facilities are free. A concerted effort can be made to establish one hour during the day for a club activity period, not just for sport clubs but for all clubs in the school.

It might be possible to arrange for community resources to be made available. Bowling alleys, rifle and archery ranges, ball fields, pools, and other areas could be freed for one or two hours per week or month for the club.

The coordinator of the club program could assist through letters, telephone calls, and personal contacts in getting facilities for club use. It is often much easier for a faculty person to make such arrangements than it is for the student.

If the club program becomes large, it may be unfeasible for the intramural department to subsidize the acquisition of equipment needed by the clubs. This is especially true if such equipment is expensive. Few schools could provide skis, rifles, scuba diving or lacrosse gear, or bows and arrows without financial support from sources outside of the department.

5. *Establish rules and regulations governing the action of the clubs*. One of the goals of the club member often is competition with other clubs in other schools. Interclub contests by high school groups are governed in many states by regulations that limit competition to recognized varsity sports

departments. Club officers and advisors should be aware of limitations on interschool club contests.

Travel inside or outside of the village, town, or city should be carefully supervised whenever the club members are traveling expressly for club purposes. Responsible adults should drive, or the advisor of the club could lead the caravan.

If both boys and girls are to go on trips, for example, a skiing weekend, proper chaperoning might be arranged, and each person must submit a permit and waiver of responsibility signed by the parent or guardian.

Special parties held at the school or elsewhere as part of the club's social programming need the permission of the school authorities, who may approve or disapprove the type and the place of the function. Such regulations may seem onerous to the club personnel, but they are for the best interests and protection of all the members. A thorough understanding of the rules will usually lead to their acceptance.

6. *Keep an evaluation system in effect.* By demanding periodic reports from the officers, the club coordinator can evaluate the progress of each group. If an organization is threatened with extinction, an attempt should be made to discover why the club isn't functioning properly or why it appears to be going defunct.

Perhaps it's possible to rejuvenate the club through getting another advisor, changing the membership regulations, eliminating or increasing dues, or holding meetings more often. A questionnaire or interviews can often reveal the reasons why the club isn't functioning as it should. On the other hand, the success of the club might have been highly dubious from the beginning, so that it might be better to cancel it entirely.

With ever-increasing numbers of students enrolling in the public and private secondary schools, a lower percentage of students will have an opportunity to play varsity sports. The only practical answer to the question of what to do with the great masses of pupils who won't get a chance to compete in varsity sports is the organization of intramural sports programs and, as an integral part of intramurals, the sport club program.

COLLEGE AND UNIVERSITY SPORT CLUBS

Perhaps the most difficult question to answer is "What responsibility does the university or college have for the administration of the sports club program?" The answer to the question depends largely upon the philosophy that the institution has regarding *in loco parentis*. Those schools which still feel that they should strictly govern the lives of the students generally keep a fairly tight rein on the activities of sport club members. Where administrators feel the need to know at all times what the students are doing, where they are going, and how they are going to get there, there seems to be an abundance of rules, regulations, and red tape tied in with the program. On the other hand, in institutions where the idea of *in loco parentis* is a thing of the past, the clubs have complete freedom in the organization and administration of their activities.

I have seen the extremes of both of these philosophies and had the opportunity to become acquainted with the club programs in many colleges and universities. It is my opinion that if sport clubs are to flourish under conditions that result in the least cost to the school, the greatest freedom of choice to the member, and the advancement of maturity of the club participants, then there should be complete freedom for the students to manage as they see fit.

Where administrators have chosen a few clubs to subsidize fully (i.e., provide all equipment, every facility, and all travel costs), the club program does not develop as fully as where the financial burden for equipment and travel costs lies with the club members. Who can decide which clubs merit help and which do not? What administrator determines which clubs should even exist on campus? Why should students have to register with an office if they wish to go on a trip? Who better can decide than the club members how much competition they should have during the year?

These days, when students are demanding a greater voice in the conduct of their affairs, a very acceptable philosophy that can be adopted by the administrators of club programs is embodied in the following principles:

1. Students should have the right to form and belong to any type of club they choose as long as the activity around which the club is centered is not an illegal one.
2. Club members should be given the right to choose their own officers, conduct their own business affairs, operate their own activities, and run their meetings as they wish.
3. Participants of sport clubs should be made aware of their legal responsibilities toward the institution, club members, and their parents or guardians.
4. Institutions should assist the clubs by providing minimum facilities, a little basic equipment when possible or feasible, and some communication medium with as little expense as possible.
5. Administrators responsible for sport club affairs should ask for some accounting of club affairs, but as little as possible.

Club programs that are organized under these suggestions have been and will continue to be thriving and healthy organizations that offer students the maximum opportunity to develop leadership, responsibility, and maturity. There is little enough opportunity on the average campus for students to be involved in the decision-making process in which they so desperately need experience. Most students have accepted the challenge to regulate their own affairs and have proven to be able to do so admirably.

Acknowledgment

This chapter was originally published as "Organizing sports clubs for secondary schools" by D.O. Matthews, 1978, *NIRSA Journal*, 3(1), 38-41. Copyright 1978 by NIRSA. Reprinted by permission.

CHAPTER 3

Organization and Administration for New Sport Club Directors

Sam Hirt
Vanderbilt University

A sport club department is an intricate establishment to develop. Although each situation is different, there are also similar factors to be addressed. The following outline is designed to guide new directors of sport clubs as they assume responsibility for club program administration on campus. These ideas have been gleaned from personal practices of many sport club supervisors.

A. *One must understand the present status of existing sport club departments before initiating changes.*
  1. Is the sport club program inherited or is it in the beginning stages of development?
     • One must understand *how, where,* and *why* the program is aligned administratively at one's institution.
     • One must establish or follow the school's regulations for chartering a new group. The majority of schools require annual constitutional renewal.
  2. One must understand that the number of clubs in operation at any one time varies from year to year. Some factors to consider that may affect the number of clubs on a campus are
     • Programs nationwide are experiencing rapid growth.
     • Many athletic departments are eliminating some athletic teams because of financial stress. These teams may attempt to become included within the sport club program.
     • Some sports based upon NCAA requirements become elevated to athletic program status.

- Movement in women's activities has been tremendous in recent years via this route, mainly because of Title IX.
- Some clubs will become inactive because of a lack of interest, poor leadership, or little or no coaching.

3. The sport club director should develop a priority plan for the usage of the facilities. This plan establishes where sport clubs are to be placed on a priority list for the reservation of recreation/athletic facilities.

- *Review all facilities.* Chart and study feasibility of usage for the different activities.
- *Assign a person(s) to be in charge of the master reservation system.* Some policies and procedures to put into effect are to visually inspect areas daily, put all maintenance needs in writing, establish sound usage policies and, if appropriate and necessary, establish a fee system to pay for maintenance.
- Explain the procedure of limiting sport clubs to a certain number of practices per week on fields, courts, or in pools.
- A red-flag policy may be set to protect the fields. When a red flag is up, fields cannot be used.
- Develop a daily maintenance schedule for the facilities.

B. *Establish and strive toward them.*

1. *Long-term goals*: Write down the individual and program priorities. Give great thought and planning to the projected ideas of director, students, staff, and the university administrators. Be patient and strive to attain worthwhile goals.

- Receive bids when possible for capital work to be done or for purchases over a certain amount of money.
- Growth should always be a long-term goal.

2. *Short-term goals*: Write down these individual and program goals and publicize them. Include the staff and students in this process, therefore promoting teamwork.

C. *Strive for total university involvement of participants, helpers, and spectators.* The total university community should be encouraged to become involved in the program. People have different expertise and most are willing to share it when solicited to help.

- Students are the base of support for the program. The needs of students are the only reason for creating the position of sport club director. When the students and the university are involved in decision making, the programs will expand, budgets will increase, and the enthusiasm will greatly increase.
- Help in budget preparation should be sought from the accounting office and the campus recreation director's staff.

- The administrative deans can speak at various club gatherings that lend themselves well to club promotion. At many institutions, these sorts of contacts with deans have helped the program when the budget for clubs was exhausted.
- Other university offices and staff members may offer suggestions for raising funds by conducting special events or contacting people and companies who might donate money to the club program.
  (1) Establish a sport club gift account fund.
  (2) Talk with club participants and encourage them to make donations to the gift account.
  (3) Solicit material goods from commercial firms that can be used by club members for club activities.
- Search out interested faculty members who would serve as faculty advisors for a club.
- Financial aid personnel in the university or college can identify potential workers to help raise money.
- Most importantly, a close working relationship needs to be developed with the school's legal office. This office can work closely with the department or club in developing the proper waiver/release forms and all other related forms.
- Because most schools depend heavily on the plant operations department, daily and weekly facility usage schedules should be sent to that administrative unit so they can coordinate their work with the program demands of the sport clubs.
- The radio and publications offices are vehicles through which it may be possible to advertise club activities. The director should develop a plan for advertising and promoting the club events.
- Security office personnel will help in emergencies and at special events if they are provided with the practice and contest schedules of the sport clubs.

If a new sport club director has access to guidelines such as these, the development of a program may be simplified. Each university's campus recreation department is unique and, therefore, may encounter problems not previously discussed. One must find solutions to problems by sharing the experiences of others.

When new sport club directors contemplate instituting a new program or improving one that is in existence, they should consider the following items as they prepare a sport club handbook for the students who are or will become involved in the administration of a sport club:

1. The *definition* of a sport club on campus.

2. The *objectives* of the sport club program.
3. Preparation of a *roster* of all clubs on campus and their funding dates.
4. A presentation of the *organizational scheme* of campus recreation and how the sport club program fits into that scheme.
5. A listing of the *specific guidelines* for the clubs should be published. These guidelines would pertain to:

   - Organization of the *governing unit* under which the clubs are established.
   - The steps to follow in *establishing* a club.
   - When club *meetings* are to be held.
   - How club members are to *conduct* themselves on and off campus.
   - What the *officers* are supposed to do and how to do it.
   - *Advisors' and coaches' roles* in the management of the club.
   - Establish in writing the *eligibility rules* for membership in a club.
   - Sound *financial practices* should be investigated and understood by all persons involved in the management of the club program.
   - *Facility usage* with a knowledge of the procedures to follow in requests for and usage of facilities.
   - An *equipment* manager for each club will be responsible for equipment purchase, storage, inventory, repair, and check-out and check-in and for setting up records for these procedures.
   - *Competition* with other clubs, if the club so desires it, demands a special set of rules and regulations, which will entail such things as transportation, meals, rooms, insurance, and liability. Club managers along with the sport club director should review appropriate contract and other agreement forms for home and away contests.
   - *Transportation* forms using university-approved policies must be filled out and filed with the appropriate office before clubs use their own cars or university vehicles.
   - *Medical care and insurance coverage* is required for the protection of the university, club director, advisors, coaches, and club members. Liability implications should be carefully considered before members participate in the club's activities.
   - *Publicity* is a vital part of the growth and development of the club program. Avenues for publicizing the program may include the following: bulletin boards, campus newspaper, telephones, demonstrations and exhibition of club activities at university athletic contests, clinics, luncheons for and with university administrators, television and radio announcements, trophy cases, and special award programs.
   - Various club *administrative forms* might include request for team affiliation, request for charter recognition, waiver and release,

club roster, travel expense forms, budget requests, facility reservation, injury reports, equipment management, and other university regulations and necessary reports and forms.

The administration of a sport club program is not an easy task, even for the experienced director. A person newly assigned to the job of supervising the sport clubs on campus should be willing to solicit all of the assistance that exists and is available. Looking to others for help in managing the program is not a sign of weakness or ineptness; rather, it is an indication of the willingness of the new director to learn from and through others who have had some experience in the sport club area.

For the new director, there is a great deal of literature on the administration of club programs. The published proceedings of the National Intramural-Recreational Sports Association (NIRSA), the articles printed in the *NIRSA Journal*, the many handbooks that are available for the asking, and the many meetings in which sport club administration is discussed all contribute to the large body of information available to the new, and the "old," sport club program director.

Acknowledgment

This chapter was originally published in *Interpretive aspects of intramural-recreational sports* (pp. 212-218) edited by B.C. Vendl, D.C. Dutler, W.M. Holsberry, T.C. Jones, and M. Ross, 1984, Corvallis, OR: NIRSA. Copyright 1984 by NIRSA. Reprinted by permission.

CHAPTER 4

Alternative Methods
of Sport Club Administration

Judy Heller
Boston University

Sandy Vaughn
University of Oregon

Sport club programs are a relatively recent entrant into the realm of campus recreation. Although sport clubs have been in existence since the early 1900s, there are no strong historical administrative structures and policies in the sport club programs today. This background allows for innovation and flexibility. Decisions may be based on current realities and needs, rather than on some codified rules in which one must search for loopholes.

The purpose of sport clubs is to fulfill the recreational, competitive, and athletic needs of the student population. The emphasis should be on student leadership, with the strength of the club based on group participation.

In every institution of higher education there exist different facilities, personnel and organizational structures, and highly diversified student populations. These differences are, in turn, reflected in institutional philosophies and goals that influence campus recreation programs. For this reason, there is not any ideal formula for sport club administration. Rather, each administrator should ideally become familiar with alternative structures in order to build a program that best meets the needs of a particular campus population.

The sport club program that seems extremely successful at a large four-year institution may be totally inappropriate at a small commuter college. For this reason, each area of sport club administration must be evaluated

in the context in which it is viewed by those who are eligible to participate in it. Questions such as the department to which sport clubs should
belong, the sources of funds, and the process by which decisions on policy
are to be made must all be considered in terms of the impact of the particular decision on the particular campus.

SPONSORING AGENCY

Sport clubs may be aligned with various departments, depending
primarily on the financial realities and physical structure of the college
campus. In many cases, the student services area or college union may
provide solid funding, as well as flexible support, for a viable sport club
program. Circumstances may provide an optimal setting for the central
sport club office in a visible place, such as the college union. However,
if a student services affiliation means that the only office available for sport
clubs would be in an obscure corner of an administration building, a sport
club program may wish to look elsewhere to provide exposure to the
opportunities which it provides.

Others have found that working with the physical education department and being housed in the physical education building greatly
strengthened their sport club programs. Financial support and equipment
and facility availability may be advantages to being aligned with the physical education department.

On other campuses, sport clubs may be administered and funded
through the athletics or general student activities fund. It is important
that those involved in the administration of the sport club program be
aware of the people to whom they report, the club's sources of funds,
and the club's own place in terms of facility priorities to be able to effectively aid clubs should they need assistance or information. The formation of individual clubs in a recreational program is generally recognized
as the responsibility of the students themselves. This is a major component that distinguishes sport clubs from an intercollegiate athletic program. This approach to club formation allows students to develop
leadership potential through active participation in both competitive sports
activities and the organization of club activities and to accept responsibility for their own contributions or the results of apathetic attitudes.

RECOGNITION AS A CLUB

The criteria for admission of a club into the sport club program may
vary as much as the types of sports to be included in such a program.
Much of this depends on the philosophical thrust and purpose of the sport

club program. A program that emphasizes competition and a winning record will definitely require different criteria than an instructional or casual club program.

For a program oriented toward meeting the competitive needs of students that are not already met by intercollegiate athletics or intramurals, a number of criteria may be used to determine if inclusion in a sports club program is appropriate. These are:

1. Student interest in the sport.
2. Availability of facilities for practice and competition.
3. Availability of adequate competition within a reasonable geographical range.
4. Availability of funds to meet the financial needs of the club.
5. Availability of a coach and/or student leader.
6. A demonstration of student leadership within the club.
7. The potential of the club to earn supplemental funds.
8. The capacity of the club to meet needs that are not currently met elsewhere in the college setting.

In some cases, a club may exist as a strong group for a number of years and then show a steady decrease in participation, student leadership, and general interest. Ideally, the sport club coordinator or advisor would investigate the reasons for this decline to determine whether it is simply a problem of weak leadership or other temporary conditions. However, if it seems that a club is simply no longer meeting the needs of a reasonable number of students, it no longer meets the criteria for a sport club. Termination of the club as a member of the central program may be appropriate, particularly if the club is receiving funds. It is up to the coordinator or committee responsible for such decisions to consider the situation and act in the interest of the students whom the program serves.

ADVISORS

The question of whether or not to require that each club obtain a member of the faculty or staff to serve as an advisor is a difficult one to answer. It is extremely important that someone provide direction and act in an advising capacity to a sport club, whether that person is a student leader, a coach, faculty advisor, or full-time employee of the university who is responsible for the management of the sport club program.

The major advantage of the system of advisors is the continuity that an advisor can provide to the program. Student leadership is subject to change on a yearly basis. Nothing is more frustrating than seeing a club that has strong leadership one year become totally apathetic the next because of ineffective student leadership. Such frustrations might result in the coordinator wishing he or she had veto power over elected officers. But ideally, a good advisor can bridge the gap from year to year, without usurping the authority of student leaders. In addition, the advisor may serve as an additional contact when communicating policies and important deadlines to the clubs.

Some programs do not require clubs to carry a faculty advisor. This philosophy is very much in line with the student development philosophy, which allows students to develop leadership potential through group decision making. Such a situation forces students to take responsibility for their decisions rather than relying on an authority figure. The club coach takes over many of the responsibilities often filled by the advisor in the other system. In both cases the coordinator or administrator plays an active advisory role.

It must be noted that, whether or not an advisor is required, the critical factor is the emphasis on strong student leadership. A faculty member or other individual who takes over the club to the extent that students are no longer the prime leaders must be reminded of the basis of the club sports philosophy, which emphasizes student leadership and participation. The range and effectiveness of the program depends on the officers and club members, rather than on the efforts of a paid professional or overzealous advisor.

CLUB COUNCILS

There are a number of alternatives with regard to responsibility for policy development, budget allocations, discipline problems, and other administrative decisions. Many club programs opt for a policy committee or governing board. There are two major reasons for this. First, the group approach to such decisions allows for a wider perspective, aiding a coordinator who might be too close to the issue to make a judicious decision. Secondly, such a committee relieves the coordinator of the sole responsibility for decisions, avoiding the "villain" status attributed to one who must make all the decisions alone.

The question of the composition of a committee or board is a bit more controversial. One type of committee is made up of student representatives from each club. This is based on the premise that such individuals will take an active interest in decisions that affect their programs. Their knowledge of the types of problems that clubs may face can help them to relate to issues often dealt with by such a committee.

The other type of committee is made up of a mixture of students and faculty not directly involved in the program as participants but nonetheless having some degree of interest in the program and/or sports in general. By coming to the club from outside, such individuals bring a different perspective to policy decisions, which allows them to be more objective in weighing the issues.

COMMUNICATION

The communication of club business, policies, and procedures may take a number of different forms depending on available finances, program structure, and coordinator preference. A manual or guideline booklet is essential. These written policies eliminate the conflicts between administration and club officers.

Putting decisions and club business in writing is another important aspect of clear communication. Scheduling of competition and facilities should always be communicated in written form to avoid misunderstandings and conflicts with other groups.

Periodic meetings with officers may be a system that works for some programs. In a commuter college situation, where students are rarely on campus at similar times, this may be impractical and unnecessary. A central gathering place or club mailboxes may fulfill communication needs more adequately. Term and annual reports may also be helpful in keeping administration and the clubs themselves abreast of the club's accomplishments.

EVALUATION

It is important that all clubs be periodically reviewed to ensure that they are attempting to operate within established philosophy or policies, taking into consideration the individual nature of each club. For example, while there may be a travel limit imposed on the clubs, a ski or kayaking team may be forced to travel beyond that limit to find competition. In any case, this review may be done in written or interview form.

FUNDING

The guidelines for funding of sport clubs is a complicated process, because there are so many variables involved. Each sport club program has unique criteria by which funds are allocated.

The primary decision is whether or not a campus recreation department is to fund a club. Some programs require a demonstration of internal self-reliance without funding for a year or two before a club becomes eligible to request funds. Others will allow partial funding for a period, increasing financial support as the club experiences growth and stability. Still another alternative is recognition alone for a club that may desire administrative assistance but requires little or no financial support.

Club budget requests are generally based on several variables: the number of years in existence, the number of club members, the relative cost of the sport, travel and equipment needs, and the length of the competitive season. The clubs themselves may draw up and submit a written budget request, providing a good development opportunity for the officers, or the coordinator may design what she or he feels to be reasonable recommendations. Passing the budget on to a committee or other individuals can help to ensure a fair allocation of funds.

Requiring a club to earn some percentage of its budget is one means of assuring that members take an active interest in the perpetuation of the club. This may be accomplished through membership dues or fundraising activities.

There is some question as to the place of national competition in the sport club program. Although the program does not stress excellence at the expense of maximum participation, it may be unfair to restrict the potential of competitors. One solution may be the provision of a contingency fund as a support system within the program for national competition. Foundations and donations might also be other sources from which a club could seek funds.

LIABILITY AND INSURANCE

In our increasing litigious society, the question of liability becomes more and more crucial to all types of recreation programs. Club sports are no exception. Particularly with such high-risk sports as mountaineering or white water kayaking or sports with a high incidence of serious injury, such as rugby and lacrosse, the avoidance of liability suits becomes a central concern. Making participants aware of the risks inherent in a particular activity is the first step in avoiding legal problems. It is crucial that the person responsible for the sport club program find out about the policy at the institution with regard to insurance and coverage for injuries or accidents as a result of participation in a sport club event.

Many schools deal with this issue by requiring that all sport club participants carry medical insurance. This may not be possible at all institutions, or the staff may not wish to institute this requirement. By recommending and not requiring that students carry insurance, programs assume that a college student is mature and responsible enough to make his or her own decision on such matters, thereby reinforcing a philosophy that stresses student development. Other programs, despite a development orientation, require the purchase of insurance by participants for the sake of protecting the program, staff, and participants against lawsuits and legal complications. Some programs purchase insurance plans to cover those who either do not elect to purchase their own policies or do not have sufficient coverage. Many schools require that all participants sign a liability waiver as a demonstration of good faith. In any case, it is most important that those who are responsible for legal and/or insurance matters at the institution be consulted or at least made aware of the policies. This step is necessary to avoid problems if an accident or injury should occur.

The flexible nature of the sport club program makes it conducive to the constantly changing needs and desires of the student community. Traditions are not a stifling factor in the administration of sport clubs, and thus they need not be restricted from seeking open communication and cooperation among college departments and community groups. Taking advantage of all opportunities and assistance can only enrich a very worthwhile program.

Acknowledgment

This chapter was originally published in *Recreational sports programming: Proceedings of the Thirtieth Annual Conference of the National Intramural-Recreational Sports Association* (pp. 105-110) edited by W. Manning and C. VosStrache, 1979, Corvallis, OR: Benton Printers. Copyright 1979 by NIRSA. Reprinted by permission.

CHAPTER 5

Negotiating for Sport Clubs Off-Campus Play Spaces

Don C. Bailey
Sue A. Robinson
North Texas State University

Sport club programs continue to increase in number on individual campuses around the nation, and existing programs are experiencing a growing number of clubs. This growth provides many challenges for sport club directors, one of which is the need for additional play space. Campus play spaces are reaching or have reached capacity utilization at many institutions, and thus a need exists to expand to less fully utilized areas and facilities in the university community.

Traditionally, campus area and facility reservation policies and procedures have allowed cooperative utilization of play spaces on a priority-of-need basis. Because of increases in campus populations, increased participation in all types of sports activities, and the beginning and/or expansion of sport club programs, the on-campus spaces are completely utilized, and in many instances, the total amount of playing time per week per participating unit has been reduced. Off-campus areas and facilities may be available in many instances to ease this problem.

A director who finds a need for additional play spaces should begin a search for off-campus resources. Several steps should be accomplished in the search process. The first is identification of agencies, institutions, businesses, and organizations with the community that could have the types of facilities needed. A search of the yellow pages in the phone book could provide an initial listing. The local chamber of commerce will often have some of this type of information available. Aerial photographs of the area, which are often available in city or county offices, can add more information on site identification. Visits with key persons in the community may yield further information. Personal visits to areas of the city can provide more first-hand information.

After identification of prospective sites, a second step is to gather information pertaining to the resources of each. Most agencies and institutions have publicity materials available upon request and these publications usually cite their area and facility capabilities. Listings can now be developed according to categories of spaces, such as swimming pools, basketball courts, soccer fields, and tracks. Another piece of information often included is hours of operation, and this should be listed with the categorized space. A listing should be developed from these materials that notes the personnel who would be most appropriate to contact for any negotiation regarding the areas and facilities involved.

After this preliminary search for information is completed, the gathered materials and data should be compiled in some type of inventory form for easy accessibility and use. Estimates should be made at this time of the prospects for successful negotiations and the expected trade-offs and compromises that could occur.

The next step is dependent upon the need for use of specific areas or facilities. When the need arises, a careful study of the prepared report is used to develop a list of agencies and/or institutions to be contacted. This list should be formulated with the following factors considered:

1. Adequacy of areas and/or facilities available to meet the specific need of the sport club program.
2. Proximity of the areas to the campus.
3. Observed current use of the areas by the agency.
4. Time periods of needed usage by the sport club involved.
5. Exact capability of the sport club to pay for the usage in either cash or services.
6. Knowledge of any past or current relationships between the university and the particular agency.
7. Speculation on possible trade-offs or compromises that could occur in negotiations with the agency.
8. Legal aspects of entering into a contract with the particular agency.

This list of agencies should be arranged in order of best prospects first. Further search for spaces may be needed at this point if few or no specific areas and facilities are identified.

When the best prospects have been identified, contact should be made with agency personnel to arrange a preliminary meeting for the purpose of discussion only. The following people should be present at such a meeting: sport club director, sport club student leader, sport club faculty sponsor, and agency personnel. These are the university people most directly in charge of the area desired and an agency person with authority to contract with the university. The sport club director should instruct the student leader and faculty sponsor before the meeting about the importance of gaining more information and of developing a friendly, honest, concerned and businesslike atmosphere for the future negotiations. The student leader and faculty sponsor should also be aware that the sport club director is the official university spokesperson at the meeting.

The meeting should begin with introductions of all persons involved and their positions in the matter. The sport club director should explain the needs of the particular club requesting playing space. The student leader and faculty sponsor may discuss the goals and objectives of the club. These should be discussed before the meeting with the sport club director so that there are no surprises in the meeting. Agency personnel should be called upon at this point to indicate their continuing interest in the needs of the club. If both parties represented are in favor of a working relationship, the elements of a contractual agreement should be worked up at this time. Elements that should be included are:

1. Specific areas and/or facilities to be used.
2. Specific times for area usage in terms of daily hours, days per week, weeks per year, and months of the year.
3. Specific conditions of usage, to include priorities of use, maintenance responsibilities, and decisions about inclement weather.
4. Services, rental fees, contributions, or other tangible payments that could be rendered in exchange for usage.
5. Complete descriptions of conditions of liability pertaining to accidents, damages, injuries, claims, and losses.
6. Terms of the contract, to include a cancellation statement requiring at least a 30-day notification period.
7. Enforceability of the contract to the extent that it fulfills the expectations of both parties. The positions of the personnel responsible for enforcement should be named.
8. Dates for contract completion, submission for signatures, and beginning enforcement. The beginning enforcement date should be included in the contract.

The agency will normally suggest that its legal representative draw up a contract containing these basic factors. The university will want to ensure enough time for its legal representatives to study the contract before submitting it for university signatures. Usually, only the chief executive of the university or that person's designated representative may sign for the university.

When the contract has been signed and is in force, a plan must be placed in effect to establish continuing positive relationships among the parties involved. The sport club director should meet with the student leader and faculty sponsor to determine what this plan should include. Basic ingredients that the sport club director could suggest at this initial meeting would be the following:

1. A written statement that indicates all of the agency and university responsibilities in the contract could be developed to be placed in the hands of all club personnel.
2. A club meeting could be planned and a date set at which the club's responsibilities could be explained and discussed.
3. The club members should be directly involved in deciding how specific responsibilities will be fulfilled and on the timetable for that fulfillment.
4. The club members should brainstorm to identify types of behaviors and events that could enhance the relationships with the agency and determine methods for causing these behaviors and events to occur.
5. The club members should develop a sound plan for meeting the financial requirements of the contract.
6. A series of communications to the agency should be planned. These would continue to state the feelings of gratitude from the club to the cooperating agency.
7. A procedure should be developed to deal with any irregularities that might occur in use of the area or in the relationship with the agency. The sport club director should be involved in an early part of this procedure.
8. A process for evaluation of the agreement results should be formulated and a timetable set for its accomplishment.

The club, its leaders, sponsors, and the sport club director must be completely aware of the significant public relations aspects of such a cooperative agreement. If taken seriously, such agreements can reflect very positively on all parties involved and pave the way for further and possibly more extensive agreements. Agreements that are not nurtured and tended, on the other hand, can result in difficulties in communication and often long-lasting negative feelings between the parties involved. Negotiations, then, always involve efforts toward positive public relations.

Several of these types of negotiations have taken place successfully at North Texas State University. The first of these ventures was with the local public schools and the Baseball Club. The university does not have baseball playing space and, therefore, needed some local field space if any home games were to be played. In this instance, Baseball Club representatives approached the high school baseball coach regarding the possibility of using the high school field, the only field in the city at that time that fulfilled regulations with regard to outfield distance. No written agreement was drawn up, and very little done to cultivate the relationship; thus after two years, public school officials ruled that the university could no longer use the field. At this time, the university entered into negotiations with the city parks and recreation department. Club leaders, the faculty sponsor, the sport club director, and the director of parks and recreation were able to decide on the elements of a contractual agreement. The legal department for the city drew up a contract that was ultimately signed by both the city and the university.

Similar negotiations have been accomplished between other agencies and other clubs. Before 1980, North Texas State University did not have an indoor swimming pool. The Scuba Club negotiated with Flower Mound New Town, approximately 12 miles from the University, to use its indoor pool for instruction and games of underwater hockey. The Soccer Club has negotiated with an individual in the city to use an open space adjacent to university property as a practice site. The Bowling Club negotiates a yearly contract with the Brunswick Holiday Lanes for both practice and contest time; this is the only bowling facility in the city. The Rugby Club and Softball Club have both entered into agreements with the parks and recreation department of the city for use of spaces for practice sessions and for contests with other institutions. The Swimming Club has negotiated through the local unit of the Amateur Athletic Union to practice at another university in the city that has an indoor pool. The Power-lifting Club has negotiated with a local health club to utilize workout space during university holidays. The Waterskiing Club has entered into an agreement with the Fort Worth Division of the Corps of Engineers for use of certain portions of Lewisville Lake and for authorization to position a jump and slalom course in the lake.

These clubs would not have been able to function without the cooperative attitudes of the various agencies mentioned. Through successful negotiations and continued positive public relations, students are able to enjoy participation in sport clubs though their activities take place outside university property.

Acknowledgment

This chapter was originally published in *Intramural-recreational sports: New directions and ideas* (pp. 236-240) edited by W.M. Holsberry, L. Marciani, and C. VosStrache, 1980, Corvallis, OR: NIRSA. Copyright 1980 by NIRSA. Reprinted by permission.

PART II

Student Development Through Sport Clubs

Reminiscent of the beginning days of sport club developments there have been many arguments about the effectiveness and dependability of student-administered sport clubs. Some argue that the average college student is not capable or mature enough to assume full control of the management of sport clubs. Another point often heard is that the very transient nature of the student population means that there is bound to be a lack of cohesiveness and continuity in club administration from year to year. This can lead to erosion of leadership and, sometimes, the complete loss of it.

The directors of campus recreation programs who are in favor of a great deal of student involvement in club operations often pose the argument that there are so few opportunities for students to become a part of the decision-making process that club officers and student coaches should be allowed to make most of the decisions that affect their clubs. With proper supervision and evaluation by the director of campus recreation, little can happen that will damage any club to the extent that it cannot remain viable as a student organization. These students are the future leaders in government, business, and education, and they should be afforded the maximum opportunity to assume responsibility for the welfare of the club and its members.

In part II, four articles have been chosen that deal with student participation in the management of sport clubs. In the first article, Judy Heller and B. Hills stress the importance and value of getting students deeply involved in the decision-making process of club management.

The second article, written by Sandy Stratton-Rusche and Glen Radde, is a summary of a personal development inventory of sport club officers. This instrument was used to determine the effectiveness of leadership development through sport club management.

In the next selection, Gerald M. Maas develops the concept that a sport club council composed of students is an effective and valuable tool and should be used by the director of campus recreation to assist in administering the entire sport club program in an educational institution.

In the last article, "Athletic Training and Coaching: A Seminar for Sport Clubs," Sue Skola Robinson stresses that the way to attract student leaders and involve them in the total sport club program is through seminars covering aspects on coaching and training of athletes for participation in the club activity.

CHAPTER 6

Club Sports: Positive Approach to Athletic Competition

Judy Heller
Boston University

B. Hills
Langston Union

The education boom of the 1960s is over. No longer are scholarships, grants, and loans a simple matter of application. Student aid is becoming a scarce commodity, which corresponds with increasingly limited federal allocations for higher education. The administration of the 1980s paints an even bleaker picture for aid to education in this decade.

As limited academic entities within the college community, both athletics and recreation are being asked to justify their existence. Where academics are seen as the primary function of institutions of higher education, the financial hatchet often falls first within the extracurricular departments of American universities. Athletics is a prime candidate for these budget cuts.

On campuses all over the United States, administrators, who are told to trim their athletic budgets, are deciding to drop certain sports from their intercollegiate programs rather than equalize their major and minor sports. In the September, 1980 issue of *The Chronicle of Higher Education* (Angus, 1980) numerous universities are cited as having dropped two or more sports from varsity status. The University of Colorado, Yale, Colgate State, and the University of California are among those listed.

The article points to a number of partial solutions to this situation. One is the move of those teams from intercollegiate/varsity to club status. "Several colleges and universities hope that the effect of the loss of varsity status will be at least partially mitigated by competition on the club level" (Angus, 1980, p. 10).

As this development mushrooms throughout the country, it will most certainly create new challenges as well as problems for the recreation professional. The issue at hand is to turn the situation into one that can be beneficial to a maximum number of students.

As these teams assume their new role of club status, they take on responsibilities and obligations that are normally handled by the administration in the case of intercollegiate sports. These additional duties outside the line of competition are where students have the opportunity to gain experience and knowledge beyond the physical demands of their sport. It is most definitely a positive situation, and should be seen as such by the club sports coordinator and recreation department director. Individuals who are elected to positions of leadership (be they club presidents, team captains or team managers) are the most obvious candidates for this learning situation.

Specifically, as a club organization, the group has to be willing to assume the added duties of scheduling facilities for practice and the competitive schedule. The club president must come to an understanding of the financial needs, the logistics, and the preparation that goes into training and traveling. "Students on club teams are responsible for running their own practices, scheduling games, and raising most of their expense money in part by attracting alumni support" (Angus, 1980, p. 10).

The officers/captains also have a certain amount of administrative work, which requires forethought and cooperation from the rest of the team. They also become a much more critical part of the structure, because they serve as the backbone of the team and the positive enforcer of the ideals of the club. To learn what it takes to make a large group tick, no matter what the activity, is a skill for which a person can be grateful. Being a leader in a group of athletes at a collegiate level is an opportunity that ideally should be available to every student. The experience a student receives through the organizational responsibilities of a club is invaluable. Skills that will be used in many different instances in future years can be developed and tested in the collegiate recreational setting. Ideally, some of these leaders will become directly involved in our field of recreation. However, they will be better prepared for any leadership position.

These student leaders should learn quickly the efficient methods of operation. One of the most difficult, yet necessary, qualities in a leader is the ability to delegate responsibility. The success of a club is often the result of many people contributing their time and knowledge rather than one person trying to do the whole job alone.

What is true of the learning possibilities for a club leader can also be said of every individual member. In a club setting, as opposed to an intercollegiate team, the success of the club is the direct result of the energies of its members. Not only does the team have to physically compete, the members also must be willing to give time to other aspects of the organizational function. This is where the system of clubs has so much to offer in contrast to intercollegiate teams. The member who has spent time with fundraising, preparing schedules, or purchasing equipment will be able to more closely identify with the team's accomplishments and will appreciate the effort that went into developing the club to this point. With this appreciation comes a sense of intense commitment and belonging, which can often exceed that of a varsity sport.

Along these same lines, it is the students themselves who are responsible for the perpetuation of the club. "On the other hand," Mr. Holgate adds, "club sports vary in quality, generally depending on the resourcefulness of the students who head them. Without an energetic leader, a club sport may nearly or completely cease to exist" (Angus, 1980, p. 10).

Not just the daily or seasonal success, but the continuity of the organization from one year to the next is on the shoulders of the individual members. In contrast, a varsity team depends almost entirely on the coach for that carryover. This sense of unity and commitment to the group gives equal importance to all members. A first- or second-year student can contribute and play as important a role in the club's perpetuation as a senior. A club that fails to respond to this demand will soon find itself on the verge of nonexistence. The survival of the fittest is an appropriate statement of the club philosophy.

Finally it must be realized that students are mature individuals, especially those who choose to spend a good portion of their nonacademic time involved in a club sport. Students are adults and deserve to be treated as such. The recreational club program offers the perfect opportunity to give real responsibilities to students. Many directors will find that people rise to the occasion and meet the demands of a club organization. Students enjoy the requirements of leadership; they are willing to try something new, and expand their commitment from simply being an athletic participant to being more fully accountable for the team's situation. This is often in direct contrast with the varsity coach, who frequently leaves the players with few tangible responsibilities other than playing. Overall, the club program can be a much more gratifying and rewarding experience for our emerging leaders.

It is evident that club sports may fill the gap between varsity and intramural recreation when schools can no longer fully support large numbers of intercollegiate teams. It is extremely important that recreation professionals be prepared to respond to this development through qualified staff, recognition for the efforts of those involved and adequate funding whenever feasible.

Recognition of the volunteer staff, which is the backbone of any sport club program, is most crucial to the perpetuation of the clubs. This volunteer staff may consist of nonstudent coaches, faculty advisors, or student officers who put so much time and effort into making the clubs function. Without these people, no professional staff member alone could maintain quality programs.

The most obvious (and most practical) way to recognize someone's efforts in this area is through financial compensation. However, this is often the very reason that a team must be dealt with as a club. Therefore, alternative means of recognition must be sought.

Many universities offer benefits to their communities that are not easily found in other environments. Tuition-free academic courses, recreation privileges, free passes, or reduced rates to cultural events—all these are possible means of thanking and recognizing the time volunteered by club sport staff. It may take some effort on the part of the professional staff to arrange these benefits, but they will be much appreciated by volunteer staff.

Another means of recognition, which is often overlooked, is positive verbal feedback. As with paid staff members, words of appreciation and encouragement are often a most effective means of recognition as well as an additional incentive.

Other ways to provide for recognition of volunteer staff are letters to appropriate university officials, end-of-year banquets, and articles in university publications that recognize their efforts. A creative staff member can expand on this list.

Sport clubs need not be seen as the stepchild of varsity athletics. The sport club program can provide valuable benefits for participants. Recreation professionals must be ready and willing to make the most of this opportunity.

Acknowledgment

This chapter was originally published in *Intramural-recreational sports: Its theory and practice* (pp. 132-136) edited by L.S. Preo, L. Fabian, W.M. Holsberry, J.W. Reznik, and F. Rokosz, 1982, Corvallis, OR: NIRSA. Copyright by NIRSA. Reprinted by permission.

REFERENCES

Angus, P. (1980, September 15). Growing deficits force colleges to eliminate some varsity sports. *Chronicle of Higher Education*, pp. 1, 10.

CHAPTER 7

Sport Club Officers
Personal Development Inventory

Sandy Stratton-Rusch
Glen Radde
University of Minnesota

Stratton-Rusch and Radde's study, conducted at the University of Minnesota, was done in an effort to discover in what ways student development (i.e., sportsmanship, people, and management skills) takes place when students are involved in the leadership of a sport club. The implications of the study are that students can benefit in several ways by participation in the management of sport clubs in college and university settings.

The results of this particular study seem to support Matthews' and Heller and Hills' contention in their articles, presented earlier in this text, that club programs offer students the maximum opportunity to develop leadership, responsibility, and maturity.

INTRODUCTION

There is more to student development in a college setting than merely acquiring information and developing skills. Experiences in the classroom, as well as out-of-class experiences, are important in this development.

A specific out-of-class environment in which development may occur is a sport club program. This feeling is finally being confirmed as we have made one of the first attempts to ascertain and record a structure or ranking of a student development process occurring in a sport club setting. This task was accomplished through a personal development inventory of sport clubs' officers at the University of Minnesota. (The inventory can be found in Figure 1 and will be referred to throughout this chapter.) The following is a presentation and analysis of some of the data from the 21 female and 32 male sport club officers who completed the survey.

ANALYSIS OF INVENTORY

The initial research hypothesis or assumption relates to the concept that differences exist between a student's experience before and during a sport club experience. In some way, it was believed, the instrument, or inventory, would quantify a great variety of previously expressed perceptions and attitudes regarding a student group and the students' opinions of a possible ongoing growth and developmental process affecting them in the sport club setting.

After the inventories were filled out and returned by the sport clubs officers, all the values were assigned particular number equivalents (e.g., *strongly disagree* [5] to *strongly agree* [1]) to aid in statistical processing. In first handling the data, we felt it would be interesting to discover whether or not there were differences between the students' pretest and posttest sport club involvement. This was done to justify exploration with the data and determine whether or not they would support the initial hypothesis.

As shown in Table 1, 75% of the respondents indicated they had been highly involved or involved in high school extracurricular activities, which might indicate a strongly motivated group of students. At least one third of the students responded positively to all questions tabulated, including "better identifying themselves as to who they are" (Question 6, People Skills). The highest positive response to a question (77%) was related to making decisions for the club's future direction and goals (Question 7, Management Skills). This might indicate a deep concern for the continuation and well-being of the club.

Fifty-seven percent of the sport club officers responded positively to Question 1, People Skills, which related to developing a greater feeling of confidence in themselves in a leadership role. The realization and belief in their ability to guide and lead is being reinforced in the sport club setting. Of the officers, 66% responded positively to bettering their communication verbally and 68% through listening (Questions 3 and 4, People Skills). This could indicate that the respondent was placed in a position to discuss issues and ideas and communicate clearly, along with learning to become more sensitive and tolerant of others' ideas and opinions. Thirty-six percent felt they had had an opportunity to improve their physical skills in their sport (Question 2, Sportsmanship Skills). This shows that students are working hard at their sport, with a dedication and desire to better themselves.

Figure 1 Personal development inventory of sport club officers

Dear Sport Club Officer:

The purpose of this Inventory is to find out whether or not you, as a Sport Club Officer, have experienced various physical, psychological, emotional, and other stages because of and during your time in office.

Previously the idea that student development occurs in the Sport Club setting has only been an assumption. As a initial start, this survey hopes to actually document whether or not student development does indeed occur.

Your honesty and concern in filling out this survey will be greatly appreciated.

BACKGROUND INFORMATION

1. Age: _____

2. Sex: M _____ F _____

3. Year in College: Fresh. _____ Soph. _____ Jr. _____ Sr. _____ Grad. _____

4. I belong to the _____ Club.

5. I have been a Sport Club Officer for _____ quarters.

6. I have been a Sport Club member for _____ quarters.

7. I helped form my Club. Yes _____ No _____

8. I spend an average of _____ administrative *hours* per *week* on my Club.

9. I spend an average of _____ participation *hours* per *week* on my Club.

10. The high school I graduated from was:

    small (50-300 people) _____ medium (300-500 people) _____

    large (600 + people) _____

11. My involvement with high school extracurricular activities was:

    Highly involved _____   Involved _____

    Indifferent _____   Turned Off _____

    Other
    (please discuss other) _____

12. Regarding my role as a Sport Club Officer, I feel my dedication is:

    High _____   Medium _____   Low _____

13. I decided to run for Sport Club Officer because:

    It seemed challenging _____   No one else would do it _____

    I wanted to better my Club _____   It would improve my resume _____

    Other
    (please discuss other) _____

14. I believe I am performing my job as a Sport Club Officer in the following manner:

    excellently _____   very well _____   good _____

    satisfactorily _____   indifferently _____   poorly _____

    Other
    (please discuss other) _____

(Cont.)

Figure 1 (Cont.)

SPORTSMANSHIP SKILLS

Please indicate your degree of agreement with each of the following statements by *circling* the answer you feel is most related to your job as a Sport Club Officer.

Through being a member of a Sport Club and an Officer, I feel I have:

	Strongly Disagree	Disagree	Neutral	Agree	Strongly Agree
1. developed a better knowledge of the rules and mechanics of my Sport.	SD	D	N	A	SA
2. improved my physical skill level and ability to play my Sport.	SD	D	N	A	SA
3. acquired the knowledge to instruct my Sport to others.	SD	D	N	A	SA
4. acquired the knowledge to officiate or referee my Sport.	SD	D	N	A	SA
5. learned the background and historical development of my Sport.	SD	D	N	A	SA
6. appreciated more the need to develop a sound, physically fit body.	SD	D	N	A	SA
7. learned my physical capabilities in my Sport.	SD	D	N	A	SA
8. learned my limitations in my Sport.	SD	D	N	A	SA

PEOPLE SKILLS

Through being a Sport Club Officer I feel I have:

	Strongly Disagree	Disagree	Neutral	Agree	Strongly Agree
1. developed a greater feeling of confidence in myself in a leadership role.	SD	D	N	A	SA
2. learned to tolerate differences in other Club members.	SD	D	N	A	SA
3. improved my ability to communicate my feelings and ideas to other Club members.	SD	D	N	A	SA
4. learned to listen better to feelings and ideas of Club members.	SD	D	N	A	SA
5. made companions, friends, socialized, had fun with other Club members.	SD	D	N	A	SA
6. identified myself better as to who I am.	SD	D	N	A	SA
7. clarified goals for my college career.	SD	D	N	A	SA

(Cont.)

Figure 1   (Cont.)

MANAGEMENT SKILLS

Through being a Sport Club Officer I have learned to:

1. conduct business meetings for Club.	SD	D	N	A	SA
2. prepare agendas for Club business meetings.	SD	D	N	A	SA
3. coordinate a practice schedule with the Recreational Sports Office.	SD	D	N	A	SA
4. promote the Club through university, business, or community contacts.	SD	D	N	A	SA
5. realize the necessity and reason for having a Club Constitution.	SD	D	N	A	SA
6. write a Constitution.	SD	D	N	A	SA
7. make decisions connected with the Club's future direction and goals.	SD	D	N	A	SA
8. conduct fund-raising activities to raise money for the Club.	SD	D	N	A	SA

9. How do you apply some of your Sport Club experiences to other aspects of your life? (i.e.: classes, meeting people, family, etc.)

_____

_____

_____

10. What is your favorite gripe about Sport Clubs?

_____

_____

_____

Thank you very much for your cooperation, effort, and time!

In Table 2, the inventories were divided according to sex to discover whether there was a significant difference between male and female officers. One difference discovered was average age—men averaged 22.4 years and women averaged 21.9 years. Only 19% of the male club officers viewed themselves as doing an excellent or very good job, whereas 57% of the females rated themselves high (Question 14, Background Information). Yet, 41% of the men, as compared to 19% of the women, felt they had identified themselves better as to who they were (Question 6, People Skills). This might indicate that, organizationally, women perceive themselves as performing better and seem to have a higher opinion of

Table 1
Calculated Percentages of Responses in the Affirmative*
of Both Sexes to the Total Sample

	Question No.	% Responded Positive
Background Information	10 (large h.s.)	51
	11 (highly involved-involved)	75
	14 (excellently-very well)	34
Sportsmanship Skills	1	42
	2	36
	3	32
	5	28
	6	30
	7	38
	8	33
People Skills	1	57
	2	49
	3	66
	4	68
	5	42
	6	32
Management Skills	1	66
	2	38
	3	55
	4	68
	5	62
	6	51
	7	77
	8	53

*Responses of *strongly agree* (1) and *agree* (2).

their ability, but men seem to sense more identity in themselves from physical participation and place more emphasis on this than administering the club. This finding might be supportive of American society, in which the male is often conditioned somewhat more than the female to learn that physical activity is an integral part of identity. The men also

Table 2
Apparent Sex Differences in the Affirmative*
Response in the Answering of Selected Questions

	Question No.	% Men	% Women
Background Information	10	56	43
	11	56	43
	14	19	57
Sportsmanship Skills	1	41	43
	2	34	38
	3	44	14
	5	28	29
	6	34	24
	7	37	38
	8	31	38
People Skills	1	66	43
	2	53	43
	3	69	62
	4	69	67
	5	34	52
	6	41	19
Management Skills	1	44	52
	2	25	57
	3	43	71
	4	59	81
	5	56	71
	6	41	43
	7	84	67
	8	47	62

*Responses of strongly agree (1) and agree (2).

showed more confidence in their ability to instruct in their sport, as seen in Question 3, Sportsmanship Skills, by a differential of 44% to 14%. This might indicate that the women were at the point at which they were becoming proficient in playing their sport, whereas men had gone beyond that point to where they felt comfortable teaching it.

Women generally scored higher under Management Skills, which indicates they might believe that they are organized. Both sexes scored par-

Table 3
Factor Analysis Results

Factors	Eigen Values	% Variance
1	6.81	53.9
2	3.51	27.8
3	2.31	18.3

ticularly high under Question 4, related to promoting the club through various contacts, with 81% of the women and 59% the men indicating agreement to the question. This might indicate that both groups are will- ing and aware of the need to obtain more members and draw attention to their club.

METHODS

The Statistical Package for the Social Sciences (SPSS) (Nie, Hull, Jenkins, Steinbrenner, & Brent, 1975) was used upon the recommendation of those in the field. The use of this book allowed us to analyze the data via factor analysis and the Guttman scaling techniques.

Factor Analysis

The exploratory factor analysis (with Varimax rotation and Kaiser nor- malization) was undertaken to reduce the questionnaire data set to see whether some underlying pattern of relationships could be organized, in some manner, to reveal a small set of factors (or dimensions).

The results of the factor analysis presented us with three major dimen- sions that would account for the variance present in the data in terms of a model of student development. These results are shown in Table 3.

To answer questions of whether an ordering could be found within this student development structure, a Guttman scaling technique was used (see Table 4). We believe we have found three developmental scales that cross the observed factorial dimensions.

After careful examination of the way the questionnaire responses were related to the factors derived from the analysis and to themselves, it was decided to name the factors in terms of selected dimensions of develop-

Table 4
Developmental Scales

Self-Identification Scale
Questions

		P6*	M4*	S2*	B10*
Scale—Items	4	X	X	X	X
	3		X	X	X
	2			X	X
	1				X
	0				

53 Cases

Coefficient of Reproducibility = 0.90
Minimum Marginal Reproducibility = 0.76
Percent Improvement = 0.13
Coefficient of Scalability = 0.56

Extrovertive Scale
Questions

		M4	P1	S6
Scale—Items	3	X	X	X
	2		X	X
	1			X
	0			

53 Cases

Coefficient of Reproducibility = 0.91
Minimum Marginal Reproducibility = 0.80
Percent Improvement = 0.11
Coefficient of Scalability = 0.56

Planning Scale
Questions

		P7	M7	S3
Scale—Items	3	X	X	X
	2		X	X
	1			X
	0			

53 Cases

Coefficient of Reproducibility = 0.95
Minimum Marginal Reproducibility = 0.86
Percent Improvement = 0.09
Coefficient of Scalability = 0.65

*B = background section; S = sportsmanship; P = people; M = management.

ment. (The actual factor plots and numerical loadings are available, upon request, from the authors.)

Because we sincerely believe that a three-dimensional construct describes a development process ongoing in sport clubs, it was advantageous to define them as follows. Factor 1 is maturation, the sum of the skills and actions that one acquires when dealing with other individuals in a sport club setting. Factor 2 is somatic, the acquisition of physically oriented skills of sports. Factor 3 is origins, the general experience acquired before college life. What is shown in the diagrams of the factorial plots is how the individual questions of the instrument (labeled in terms of their section) relate, in terms of direction and distance, to the probable three-dimensional factor model to describe a student's development via a sport club setting.

DISCUSSION

With these tools, we are looking for an underlying structure to help us quantitatively document student development within the sport club setting. The factor analysis allowed us to assume that an underlying structure existed within the data set. We feel the factors are usable because they encompass not only sport clubs officers' growth, but more likely, human growth in general. An awareness of these factors allows programming to take on a "feeling" sports experience approach long advocated by the university recreational sports office. This means the program staff provides minimal administrative foundation and maximum assistance to the student in need of direction to foster the greatest growth for the participating individual.

The Guttman Scales that were found exemplify certain specific characteristics, and so they have been named the Self-Identification Scale, the Extrovertive Scale, and the Planning Scale. These reflect the original criteria most appropriately.

The Self-Identification Scale consists of four major components (see Table 4). The first is the participant's high school size, (Question 10, Background Information), the second is improvement of physical skills (Question 2, Sportsmanship Skills), the third is promotion of the club in the university and business areas (Question 4, Management Skills), and the final component is better self-identification (Question 6, People Skills). We offer this scale as a potential structure that may indicate the ordering of these responses in terms of a developmental process with self-identification being the objective of the responses given.

The Extrovertive Scale (see Table 4) consists of three components. The first is a greater appreciation of a physically fit body (Question 6, Sportsmanship Skills), the second is promoting the club through the university

(Question 4, Management Skills), and the third concerns the development of a greater feeling of confidence in the leadership role (Question 1, People Skills). This process is representative of two conditions needed for an individual to feel confident in a leadership role; these are the physical aspects of the sport and setting goals.

The Planning Scale consists of three major components. The first is making decisions connected with the club's future direction and goals (Question 7, Management Skills), the second is clarifying individual goals for a college career (Question 7, People Skills), and the third is the acquisition of knowledge to instruct others in the sport (Question 3, Sportsmanship Skills).

It must be emphasized here that though the scales presented are not absolutes, their main utility is that they present an ordering of responses and therefore yield a structure in terms of underlying development. Only the relative positions of selected criteria can be determined (because distance cannot be inferred at this time).

With these three scales and the supplementary information, we offer, very tentatively, a super scale that has not been adequately tested. This scale definitely yields a structure for development and might be used in a modeling process. We believe this to be a five component scale. The first component is the realization and appreciation that everyone needs a physically fit body and becomes involved in sport clubs of his or her choice according to previous experience. The second component finds the individual expressing his or her interest in developing a physically fit body through sport club membership, and, because of the emphasis placed on student management of the sport club, an individual then becomes involved in the determination of his or her club's future. Because of the student's involvement in the planning aspect of a club, as well as a commitment in terms of time and expertise to that club, we reach the third component of the scale, achievement of confidence on the part of the participating individual. The individual's confidence now extends itself, and not only do administrative capabilites improve, but there is a greater emphasis on the physical (technical) aspects of the club and of the sport, the fourth component. Confidence is further expressed in terms of competence and how articulate students are in their individual club setting. Not only can they do the job, but they are more effective and can demonstrate it to others, thus the fifth component.

IMPLICATIONS

Student development is an important process that, in terms of sport club officers, can be separated into three major dimensions within which certain identifiable structures exist.

We also offer a very tentative developmental structure that might be evidence for a new model of development or evidence for proving previous models. (See T.H.E. Model—A Student Development Model for Student Affairs, for a previous model.)

Acknowledgment

This chapter was originally published in *Theoretical and operational aspects of intramural sports* (pp. 306-316) edited by T.P. Sattler, P.J. Graham, and D.C. Baily, 1978, West Point, NY: Leisure Press. Copyright by NIRSA. Reprinted by permission.

REFERENCES

Nie, N.H., Hull, C.H., Jenkins, J.G., Steinbrenner, K., Bent, D.H. (1975). *Statistical package for the social sciences*. New York: McGraw-Hill.

T.H.E. *Model*. (1978). (Available from S.A.C. Office, University of Minnesota.)

CHAPTER 8

The Sport Club Council:
A Vital Administrative Tool

Gerald M. Maas
University of Wyoming

The administration of a sport club program can be a tedious, time-consuming, and difficult task if the clubs are not united to formulate an organized body. Attempting to coordinate the sport club program by interacting with each club individually leads to a redundancy problem of the nth power. This system also makes student input in operating the program difficult and complicates basic administrative tasks. This is further confounded by the wide variety of activities included in the definition of sport, which places the sport club director in a precarious position when he or she tries to develop one set of guidelines for the program.

The establishment of a sport club council (SCC) can put the needed structure into the sport club administrative pattern while allowing the objective of self-management of individual clubs to carry over to the overall coordination of the club program. The SCC consists of representatives of all recognized sport clubs on campus and functions in a direct advisory capacity to the sport club director. Student government and student affairs/services representation might also be appropriate for the council. The sport club director should be an integral part of the administrative structure of the university in terms of responsibility and authority. However, the administration of the sport club program should be participant centered, because this is one of the values of the individual club involvement. The SCC can provide structure for this to occur.

The most obvious and important benefit of the SCC is communication—both between the director and the clubs and between the clubs themselves. Group meetings of club representatives provide regular interaction between them, which leads to a sense of unity and *esprit de corps*. The council structure allows the director to obtain crucial club input on topics germane to the club program. These include club recognition, eligibility for club membership, financial support, facility coordination and reservation, travel, legal liability, and records of club activities as major discussion/decision-making points. The SCC should discuss these matters of importance and come up with recommendations to the director. If this procedure is not followed, the director is left to make decisions without the guidance of club members. The SCC allows the clubs to have input into the actual implementation of the club program while it provides a structure for the process.

The SCC should have formally stated, written procedures to follow or a constitution with bylaws. The constitution should specifically cover the following points:

1. The purpose of the council in statement form
2. Requirements for membership on council
3. Voting privileges for council members
4. Role of sport club director on the council (e.g., voting, nonvoting, ex officio)
5. Student government representation
6. Student affairs/services representation
7. Elected officers for the council, including president, vice president, secretary, and treasurer, with specific duties for each officer clearly stated
8. Amendments or changes in the constitution and bylaws, with procedures for these changes listed.

Other points to consider covering in the constitution could be listed as bylaws and include more specific items such as procedures to follow for recognition of a club, club registration, rosters of club members, dropping club recognition, financial support of clubs including budget preparation, approval of budgets and financial reports, participation summaries of club activities, SCC meeting attendance rules, number needed for a quorum, rules for meeting (Robert's Rules of Order), and election of SCC officers including timing of election, nomination procedures, voting procedures, and terms of office.

In summary, the SCC can be a most effective administrative tool in the operation of a sport club program. It allows for maximum input by club members into the overall coordination of the program, especially on difficult items such as club recognition, eligibility rules, budgeting, and facility reservation and use. These functions are difficult for a director to summarily decide without advice from the clubs. The SCC provides the structure that expedites this club input, and it should result in a sport club program that will be relevant to the students and have the flexibility to remain that way. Stated another way, the SCC results in a program that is essentially "of students, by students, and for students."

Acknowledgment

This chapter was originally published as "The sports club council—A vital administrative tool" by G.M. Mass, 1979, *Journal of Physical Education and Recreation*, **50**(3), 45. Copyright 1979 by American Alliance of Health, Physical Education, Recreation and Dance, 1900 Association Drive, Reston, VA 22091. Reprinted by permission.

CHAPTER 9

Athletic Training and Coaching:
A Seminar for Sport Clubs

Sue Skola Robinson
North Texas State University

Motivation training and conditioning for sport club members usually comes from the club members themselves. However, for a meeting that is different from the regular business meeting, why not provide the clubs some advice by which to improve the members as individuals and to benefit their clubs in general?

Most clubs at some point have problems in motivating club members, attracting new members, and holding the interest of regular members. Knowledge of the best method to condition the members for their particular sport is sometimes unavailable. Often the club leaders do not have time to train or motivate their club members.

A lack of enthusiasm and decreasing numbers of club leaders attending the regular business meetings calls for new ideas from sport club directors. To attract the student leaders and involve them in the total sport club program, seminars covering aspects on coaching and training athletes can be set up for the clubs.

Three areas of coaching and training discussed here are motivation, relaxation, and conditioning. A series of seminars can be presented on these areas by experts in sport psychology, physical education, or psychology. Sport club directors who are provided with the necessary materials and knowledge can discuss these areas in sport club meetings, thereby expanding the typical meeting beyond business concerns or allocating funds. The following material is excerpted from the *North Texas State University Club Sports Manual: Athletic Training and Coaching*.

Group motivation and psychological considerations for coaching are areas that are important to discuss before the physical training of the athlete. The coach and team/individual must first develop a desire for group success. The following items must be included in the discussion:

1. Emphasize the importance of pride in the group and its sources and consequences for the team.
2. Make sure that each member understands that his or her contribution to the team is valued.
3. Use various means to underscore how each teammate depends on the work of each other.
   - Each player's role on the team should be clearly defined and the importance of his or her contribution to the productivity of the team emphasized at all times.
   - Teammates must respect, trust, and believe in the capabilities of each other.
4. Group unity should be emphasized, with the reminder that the score is a product of team effort.
5. Select goals that are attainable, realistic challenges. Don't be afraid to change goals that are found to be unreasonable, difficult, or easy.
6. Encourage talk within the group about how performance can be improved or how practice can be made more stimulating.
7. Once goals have been set, consider what obstacles might prevent fulfillment of these goals and how these obstacles might be overcome by the team.
8. There must be mutual respect for the capabilities, opinions, and feelings of others.

Understanding team and individual morale and the problems causing poor morale is the first step in attaining successful group relationships. Several reasons for poor morale in a group are as follows:

1. Responsibility and leadership may be concentrated in too few hands.
2. The group may have poorly defined goals, roles and program, resulting in aimless behavior.
3. There may be too much emphasis on skill development with very few or no socializing activities to induce interpersonal attraction.
4. There may be no hierarchy of status in the group, so that the younger and new members have no one to look up to.
5. The leader may be admired, but not liked.
6. The group may be composed largely of individuals who fail to identify with each other's accomplishments or struggles.
7. There may be poor communication among athletes and between coach and athlete.

Knowledge of the reasons for a particular group's poor morale is necessary. The second step to achieving group success is to improve the group's morale. This may be possible by utilizing one or several of the following exercises in psychological skills:

1. Give individuals responsibility and a chance to express themselves creatively. Responsible involvement leaves group members with a feeling of pride in accomplishing organizational goals.
2. Try to merge the skills, ideas, feelings, and resources of members within the group. Do not try to change or mold individuals; rather, change the way the system is being managed.
3. Be aware of informal vs. formal structures. Interpersonal bonds cement groups together. Behind or within all formal organization, there is an informal, interpersonal organization that greatly affects the functioning of the formal organization. Therefore, do not ignore or push aside persons who have informal prestige or status. Provide democratic control and management by distributing leadership throughout the group. Individuals with high prestige and interpersonal status should be utilized as leaders within the formal structure. Provide channels of communication whereby official leaders can and do keep in contact with group members' attitudes and opinions. Furthermore, provide official avenues of communication for the expression of ideas, evaluations, and criticisms rather than through underground or antagonistic cliques.
4. Provide many opportunities for socializing events outside the work group. Develop a purpose outside the immediate group interest to give the group more social significance and to unify members on some common objective.
5. Seek grails rather than try to slay dragons. If you wish to inspire confidence in people, don't focus solely on failure. Rather, reflect on achievements that have already been gained. Make alternative systems attractive by building hope and inspiration.
6. Utilize role-playing or social-mirroring techniques to alleviate the problem by actually acting out sources of conflict:

   • Utilize the resources of group members to find solutions to their problems.
   • Re-enact problems and utilize meaning analysis to resolve conflict.

   The idea behind role-playing is that it helps individuals recognize what type of impression their behaviors make on others. Furthermore, it helps people see another individual's point of view.
7. Hold team meetings to allow both positive and negative feelings to be expressed openly and honestly!
8. Recognize individuals who contribute to group goals.

MOTIVATION, GOAL SETTING, AND SELF-CONFIDENCE

Motivation is a drive within an individual that arouses, directs, and energizes a player's goal-directed behavior. Motivation should be conceptualized along two basic dimensions: *direction*, the goal one is working toward, and *intensity*, how hard one is trying to reach the intended goal.

Goals provide direction, allow evaluation of progress, and represent a motivational factor that guides behavior and gives it its purposeful character. Thus, goals provide standards to inspire us to do our best and to find out what we are and what we are not.

The ability to set specific goals and pursue them in a systematic way separates those who want to excel from those who actually do. The question arises, "How can we use goals to build self-confidence within our young athletes?" Goals should be challenging yet realistic and attainable. A series of short-term goals that relate to long-term goals should be established, with specific target dates for achievement. Following is a list of sample goals:

Long-Range Goals	Short-Range Goals
1. Winning season	1. One game at a time; keep to the game plan and minimize physical and mental mistakes.
2. Desire to reach .500	2. Strive to win two games in a row on the road; play at least .600 ball at home.
3. Desire to hit .300	3. Strive to consistently hit the ball hard.
4. Lower ERA	4. Try to pitch a shut-out or allow only one earned run a game.
5. Strive for excellence and reach potential	5. Strive for consistency and learn from mistakes. Immerse yourself in a feeling of flow.

While long-range goals act as an incentive or guide for action, the attainment of previously set short-term goals creates a growing sense of confidence, personal accomplishment, and self-satisfaction within an athlete. Therefore, if athletes can set subgoals just far enough ahead as to require continuous improvement and effort, but not so far ahead as to be unreachable, then the corresponding success will build confidence in their capabilities.

The urge to do one's best, to excel, is a part of a constant urge for self-improvement. Pride, poise, perseverance, and patience are key attributes associated with successful performance. Worthwhile things come from hard work and careful planning. Therefore, concentrate on your objective and be determined to reach your goal. You'll be satisfied when you get there!

ANXIETY, AROUSAL, AND COMPETITION

Anxiety and arousal are natural components of competitive athletics and have a direct effect on one's attentional processes. Anxiety may be broken down into two major components: a worry component (i.e., a cognitive concern over performance) and an emotional component (physiological arousal).

When one's mind is disturbed by anxiety or self-doubt, the expression of one's potential becomes hindered, which leads to an increase in mental mistakes. This leads to overtrying. Overtrying is usually expressed in terms of overtightness. Inevitably, there is an involuntary tightening of the muscles that interferes with the flow and execution of an appropriate response. The response is triggered by self-doubt and is magnified in those situations we think matter the most. This inner dialogue can only serve to worry or distract an athlete. What is needed is not a self-doubting, worried mind, but an alert, concentrated, well-focused mind. Relaxation and concentration are interrelated. You should want your body relaxed, but ready; your mind should be calm, but focused. Relaxed concentration is a learned art that must be practiced to be perfected.

HOW TO RELAX

Relaxation training is teaching the athlete how to command specific muscles to relax. A tension-relaxation exercise can be used before and after competition. The exercises are, by nature, designed to increase flexibility, which is a key ingredient in all sports activities.

The tension-relaxation program (T-R) is easy to administer, easy to understand, and easy to accomplish. The hardest part of the entire program rests with the individual's mental capacity to concentrate on one area of the body at a time. First, the different muscles are tensed and then relaxed. Once the body's muscles have gone through this first phase, then a total body relaxation method is instilled, leaving all of the muscles as relaxed and motionless as possible. When this technique is used to go to sleep, most people, after some practice, are asleep before they have completed the program.

To begin, a warm, quiet place should be chosen, where there are as few people around as possible and where one can go undisturbed for approximately 30 minutes.

Next, the individual is told to remember to concentrate on one body part at a time, placing all other thoughts, good and bad, out of the way. Twenty minutes should be allowed for the completion of this exercise.

The individual lies faceup, making sure to never hold the breath at any point in the exercise.

1. Tighten the muscles around the eyes, nose, and mouth. Hold this tension from 5 to 10 seconds to begin with, then relax. Feel these specific muscles "let go," with no feeling of control. (Wait up to 15 seconds before going to step 2.)
2. Tighten the muscles of the neck for the same amount of time. Feel the tension build, then relax completely as in step 1.
3. Tighten the muscles in the chest and shoulders, then relax.
4. Tighten the muscles in the upper and middle back, then relax.
5. Tighten the muscles in the upper arms, lower arms, and hands, then relax.
6. Tighten the muscles in the stomach and lower back, then relax.
7. Tighten the muscles in the hips, then relax.
8. Tighten the muscles in the upper legs around the knees, then relax.
9. Tighten the muscles in the lower legs and ankles, then relax.
10. Tighten the muscles in the feet and the toes, then relax.

All coaches might be interested in knowing the number of students who are lying awake at home in bed after practice or competition because they are still keyed up and do not know how to unwind.

CONDITIONING

One aspect of conditioning, that of summer training, must be understood by those clubs which continue to practice during the summer months. Knowledge in motivation and relaxation is important; however, training and conditioning information is basic to all sport professionals.

Winning isn't everything; however, feeling good about one's skills as a result of correct training and conditioning can add to the athlete's self-esteem and the group's morale.

To help protect club members from mistakes that are commonly made by athletes and fitness buffs, the following list is provided. By following these statements, athletes may participate safely and compete more effectively in their sport during hot weather.

1. A person needs extra conditioning to exercise in the heat.
2. A person needs to train specifically to exercise in the heat and high humidity.

3. A person cannot perform as well in hot as in the cold weather and must learn to hold back early to have some energy left in reserve.
4. Do not replace salt lost in sweating by taking salt tablets.
5. Potassium and magnesium, not salt, are the minerals that the body needs in hot weather.
6. Drink as much liquid as desired.
7. Drink cold drinks (40 °F) rather than lukewarm because cold liquid is absorbed faster into the bloodstream.
8. Do not take drugs.
9. Wear white clothing to reflect the sun's rays. Clothing should be solid enough to block the sun's rays and porous enough to allow evaporation. Wear covering on the head because 20% of body heat is lost through the head.

Clubs are becoming more competitive and specialized in their particular sport. Athletic training and coaching are areas that are necessary to include in sport club meetings or seminars, and they have been neglected in the past. Psychology, physical education, and sports psychology departments, with their expertise in physical training and psychological training, are fantastic resources. Sport club professionals need to expand sport club program offerings and use these available resources.

Acknowledgment

This chapter was originally published as *Intramural-recreational sports: Its theory and practice* edited by L.S. Preo, L. Fabian, W.M. Holsberry, J.W. Reznik, and F. Rokosz, 1981, Corvallis, OR: NIRSA. Copyright 1981 by NIRSA. Reprinted by permission.

Portions of chapter 9 were contributed by David Yukelson, Hermann Hospital, Center for Sports Medicine, Houston, Texas.

PART III

Sport Club Financing and Fund-Raising

S port clubs have traditionally been self-sustaining organizations in that members of clubs were asked to assume almost all of the costs of the operation of their club activities. Over the years, a number of institutions have provided some basic equipment and scheduled on-campus facilities for the clubs, but in general club programs have not been subsidized to any great extent by colleges and universities.

The financing of sport clubs is still one of the crucial issues in sport club administration, and one that cannot be easily resolved. Careful planning and astute husbanding of departmental and club monies are needed to effectively finance the club program so that the maximum amount of funding is provided to as many clubs as possible.

If clubs are to operate on a sound financial footing, the club members must work closely with the director of campus recreation or with the sport club council, if one exists.

A 1982 sport club survey revealed that 81% of the clubs surveyed assessed dues as a prerequisite to club membership. The amount of these dues ranged from $2 to $40. In 64% of the institutions responding some partial funding existed for the clubs through student fees that were assessed upon all students. In addition to the fees and membership dues, 48% of the administering departments for the club program allocated some departmental funds to the clubs. Finally, 85% of the clubs were involved in fund-raising projects, which included soliciting gifts from various persons. (See chapter 16.)

Each of the three articles in part III provides a different perspective on the important issues of club financing. In "Fund-Raising: Getting Down to the Nitty-Gritty," Patti R. McNeeley and Loretta Capra emphasize the fact that fund-raising is a crucial part of many sport club programs. Within the article they give a number of procedures to follow in raising funds and conclude that fund-raising events can be fun as well as financially rewarding.

The second paper was presented initially at the first national conference for sport clubs held at the University of Illinois in 1977. Larry Cooney of Iowa State University prepared this comprehensive article for that conference and has recently updated it for this publication.

The final selection is a set of guidelines concerning funding sport clubs at The Citadel. The Sport Club Council decides what amount of money each club will be allotted and is made up of the faculty sponsor or coach of a club along with one student representative from each of the sport clubs.

CHAPTER 10

Fund-Raising: Getting Down to the Nitty-Gritty

Patti R. McNeely
University of Colorado

Loretta Capra
Colorado State University

Fund-raising is a crucial part of many recreational programs, especially in the area of sport clubs. This paper will deal with planning and hosting fund-raising events as well as evaluation and follow-up after the event. Although emphasis will be on fund-raisers for sport club programs, these ideas will apply on a broad basis to any fund-raising activities.

Long before the actual date of the event, a planning process begins and must be carried out if the event is to be successful. Identification of purpose, goals, and objectives should be dedicated as they relate to (a) the type of exposure that the organization is hoping to gain, (b) how much money is needed and realistic to expect, (c) whether or not the fund-raiser will be directly related to the sport club or organization hosting it, (d) how cohesive the group hosting the event is (Can they expect total participation from the membership, and will the event help develop a feeling of working together toward a common goal within the group?), and (e) whether community awareness is desired and if so whether this fund-raiser will help attain that end.

Next, a consideration of the possible types of fund-raisers opens up unlimited possibilities. What type of activity is desired and feasible? Should it be an indoor or outdoor event? This requires taking into account the weather at that particular time of year as well as the type of activities most likely to be successful for the general climate and surroundings of the area. Should it be an active or passive event—are people more likely to want to participate or watch?

A review of past events and their success is important at this time. Consider the feasibility of a suggested event for your particular group and surroundings. Take a look at what facilities are available and whether they are appropriate in terms of spectators or participants, parking, safety, and security. What is an appropriate date? For example, are there other popular events in the area on that same date (holidays, etc.)? A break-even point must be established to decide if the fund-raiser will be cost-effective. Can the group afford to take a possible loss the first year until the event is established? How many people can be counted on to be involved? Do you need many or just a few to make the event work? It wouldn't be feasible to try to schedule an event that required many volunteers when you only have a sponsoring group of 10. Is the group an active one, or do they wait for someone else to do the work for them? Is the activity appropriate to the geographical area and does it consider current trends? Also, is the area open to a new or novel idea (would a punk rock dance work in a redneck area)? All these factors must be taken into consideration along with the appropriate time and day of the event (an afternoon and night in the middle of the week wouldn't necessarily be appropriate for a beer party).

Once you have decided on an event, it is time to PREPARE! To ensure one person doesn't get stuck doing all the work, select a fund-raising committee. Choose a chairperson and assign individual duties to get things rolling. A timetable, if followed closely, can make all the difference in the world when it comes to following up on what is being done toward preparing for the date of the event. Once tasks are assigned and workers identified (volunteer or paid), it is necessary to communicate with these people and let them know what is happening. Regular meetings allow for follow-up in all areas.

One of the major and most intricate parts of the preparation stage involves creation of a budget. Depending on the type of event, you may have to have "front money" available. Many organizations are unable to spend or commit any money they don't actually have, and this can be a problem. What are the initial layout costs? If they are more than the group can handle, a commercial sponsor or backer might be necessary. What are your institution's purchasing procedures? Do you need to order large purchases months in advance? Is petty cash available, and in what amounts? What are facility costs and security deposits? Are there costs or deposits on performers or entertainment? Is special insurance necessary for a spectator event or liability coverage? How will you pay for awards, prizes, advertising, tickets, hospitality foods for the entertainers, participants, and worker crews? What is your projected income and net profit?

After identifying all of your monetary needs, you can progress to scheduling facilities and security for the event. Are the available facilities adequate for your needs, taking into account size, lighting, parking, accessibility, and safety? What type of security is necessary? Are building supervisors and/or proctors provided with the rental or scheduling of the facility? Are additional security (rent-a-cops, club personnel, etc.) needed and available? Parking lot attendants can also be a crucial consideration in the hosting of a large event.

Legal aspects can become particularly tricky if you don't consider them from the start. What types of contracts will be needed for hosting the event? Facility, performer, entertainment, advertising, commission sales, and worker agreements are all possible contracts that should be drawn up and approved by the institution's legal counsel in advance so that potential loopholes are taken into account.

It is important in the preparation of a contract to make it a legally binding contract (university or institutionally approved); require payment by percentage or consignment; indicate time, date, type of event; specify return policies; provide for cancellations by either party; set rain dates; determine amounts; and define payment procedures.

The institution may have certain regulations that would affect the particular event and its preparation. In the case of a sale of some sort you must also consider charging state and city sales tax and getting permits in advance. Liquor licenses take time and must be obtained for any event where alcohol will be sold. What about sanitation regulations for bake sales, provision of portable toilets for concerts or very large events? Insurance must be considered along with the contract end of any event— field or facility insurance, liability for participants and/or spectators, medical liability, and/or the use of waiver forms. Damage insurance is a good idea for a particularly rowdy group such as a rugby party.

Although the ideal way to get workers is to have them so dedicated to the event and organization that they would jump at the chance to help out, unfortunately that isn't always the case. So, we pursue other incentives to get them involved. One method of working with sport clubs or other organizations is to require a work deposit at the beginning of the season, which will be returned when a certain level of participaton is carried out through involvement in fund-raising events or other mandatory events. Other ways to get members motivated to put forth an all-out effort are providing free admission to an event for cleaning up afterward, being involved in some other way in the preparation of the event, giving free tickets to other events (free lift tickets for another day of skiing if they work a ski race), and awarding commissions or prizes for the most sales or a certain amount of sales.

Without advertising and promotion, success of any event will be limited, so it is important to pursue this area in detail. There are a vast number of ways to draw attention to your cause without spending much money. Press releases, public service announcements, campus calendars, articles in local and campus papers, and flyers spread around campus can all give good exposure for little or no cost to the organization. Other promotional techniques include buttons, t-shirts, bookmarks, matches, and pins, mailings, free tickets given away on local radio stations, and advertising and posters on and off campus. Originality and creativity are needed to spark ideas for demonstrations or attention getters to promote your event. Commercial sponsorship to cover advertising or printing costs will often provide excellent exposure to both the sponsor and the event as well.

The last major area in the preparation for the event is ticket sales. Tickets must be ordered or printed and should be numbered to permit accurate accounting procedures. Color coding for various nights or prices (advance sales, etc.) can also help. Advance sales can be done in a variety of ways: by the club members, or out of the administrative office, a university box office, or athletic ticket office, or off-campus ticket service. Receipts may be required and should be taken into account. A cash box and change fund should be arranged for in advance along with security pick-up of large amounts of cash and the deposit of funds to prevent theft or potential problems.

As the date of the event approaches, setup and takedown should be arranged. Depending on the event, this can either be very simple or quite complex. Volleyball standards, bleachers, timing equipment, lights, public announcement and sound systems, locker and towel sign outs for visiting athletic teams, trainers, emergency care, ambulance attendants, clean-up crews, and lockup and security should all be arranged.

Eventually all events must come to a close, but the work isn't finished yet. During the evaluation and follow-up, accounting must be done to determine the money raised, to pay bills and labor, and to evaluate the financial success of the event. It is important to take into account exposure gained and overall benefits as well as monetary gains. Determine what records should be kept (results, entry cards for mailing lists, etc.). Acknowledgment and thank-you letters to sponsors, donors, workers, and so forth should be done at once. A written evaluation that includes positive or effective aspects, problems and possible solutions, and changes to make the event run smoother next time are extremely advantageous when it comes to planning for the next event.

If all this sounds like a lot of hassle, it can be! But it doesn't have to be if you are prepared and consider the possible problems in advance. Don't rely on one person to do all the work. Delegate the various tasks involved in the process to a fund-raising committee, and you will find that hosting a fund-raising event can be fun as well as financially rewarding.

CHECKLIST FOR SPONSORING A FUND-RAISER

Budget

Availability of "front money"; commercial sponsors; purchasing procedures; facility costs; security deposits; entertainment deposits, special insurance; awards, prizes; advertising costs; tickets; hospitality foods; worker crews.

Scheduling and Security

Door admission arrangements; adequate facilities (size, lighting, safety); special arrangements (setup and takedown); building security schedules; additional security (rent-a-cop, etc.); club security people.

Setup and Takedown

Adequate help; seating—bleachers, and so forth; equipment—volleyball standards, timing equipment, and other items; locker arrangements/ towels; trainers/emergency care; ambulance; cleanup crew.

Contracts and Legal Aspects

State and city regulations; university regulations; state all possible problems in contract (legally binding; payment by percentage or consignment; time, date, type of event; return policies; cancellations by either party; rain dates; amounts; and payment procedures.); type of contracts (facility; performer; entertainment; advertising, commission sales, and worker agreements.); insurance and liability.

Incentives

Work deposits, tickets to events or other tickets, commissions, prizes for most sales or work.

Advertising and Promotion

News releases, paid advertising (campus paper, city papers, radio), posters on campus and off, radio public service announcements, television (sports) if feasible, news articles, word of mouth, flyers buttons, t-shirts, and so forth.

Ticket Sales

Advance sales, cash box, security pickup of money.

Evaluation

Problems, changes for next time, exposure gained, written evaluation, benefits—was it worth it?

FREE PROMOTION

1. Press releases to local papers (allow two weeks notice), radio announcements of free or nonprofit events.
2. Public address announcements in high schools (allow two weeks notice).
3. Notify local clubs and organizations having similar interests.
4. Notify campus calendars.
5. Announce at residence halls during meal hours.
6. Paint banners for on campus (obtain approval from campus authorities).
7. Set up a booth on campus (student union, etc.) with proper approval.
8. Chalkboards in classrooms, chalk on sidewalks with the program, time, date, and place.
9. Various free advertising available on campus (check with campus paper).
10. Announcements at sporting events (through athletic department) and campus productions.
11. Dress up in costume (appropriate if related to event) and walk around campus, student union, especially during noon hour.
12. Telephone names out of the directory.
13. Public service announcements.
14. Local businesses.

TECHNIQUES IN ADVERTISING

1. Flyers are a great way to advertise quickly; tack them up around dorms and campus, but check first about regulations guiding this—usually only on bulletin boards.
2. Buttons—put your name, event, or catchphrase somewhere people will readily see it: coats, belts, hats, and so forth.
3. Posters—get an artist to come up with an eye-catching way to attract attention to your event. Place posters in heavily traveled areas to get maximum public awareness.
4. T-Shirts—use your logo or poster design on a t-shirt to advertise

your event or group. Sell them for $1.00 above cost and create a moving network of advertising.

5. Bookmarks, matches, and pins—useful items that can be handed out and used as reminders of your organization.
6. Mailing lists are available through various campus organizations; mail to dorms or incoming freshmen, but check with housing on regulations.
7. Free tickets to your event can be raffled away or offered by local radio stations.
8. Advertising in student and local newspapers and radio stations; can be inexpensive and reach a large number of people.
9. Local businesses might publicize or subsidize your program in exchange for giving them advertising in your progams.

(Adapted from *Student Organization Resource Manual*, Colorado State University, 1981-1982.)

FUND–RAISING IDEAS

Sports show; Casino Night/Las Vegas Night; raffles; bingo; silent or regular auction; movies/speakers; pro-am tournaments; donations of money or equipment; garage sale/ski swap or sale; commercial sponsorships; various marathons (with pledges)—swim-a-thon, skate-a-thon, dance-a-thon, jog-a-thon; Roller-Beer Bash, Rent-a-Student; spectator ticket sales/season tickets; advertising sales; trips (recreational); bake sales; program sales; car washes; candy sales; cleaning contracts; work contracts; club exhibitions; craft sales; officiating; clinics; tournaments; birthday cake service; coupon book sales or sponsorship; concerts/dances, formal or informal; banquets; plant sales; instruction programs; all-nighters; sponsoring outside groups on campus; racquet-stringing service; flea markets; sports stores; concession at events; souvenir sales—t-shirts, posters, uniforms, bumper stickers.

Acknowledgment

This chapter was originally published in *Process and concepts in recreational sports* (pp. 213-219) edited by B.G. Lamke, M.P. Holmes, W.M. Holsberry, and S.C. Meyers, 1983, Corvallis, OR: NIRSA. Copyright by NIRSA. Reprinted by permission.

CHAPTER 11

Sport Club Financing Procedures

Larry Cooney
Iowa State University

Sport clubs have developed rapidly across many university, college, and high school campuses in the United States. Over the years sport clubs have developed a philosophy of independence and self-sufficiency. Mueller and Reznik (1979) state that the characteristics of sport clubs that make them unique are self-motivation, self-administration, self-financial support, and self-regeneration. This philosophy may arise partially because many sport clubs have had difficulty finding an administrative home and financial assistance.

According to surveys by Palmateer (1979), Sliger (1978), and Phelps (1970), persons across the country responsible for sport club administration tend to agree on the following general financial practices:

1. Sport clubs should receive some funding. This may range from a few dollars to thousands of dollars.
2. Most clubs should be largely financed by club members.
3. Sources of funding should include departmental funds and/or student fees as well as gate receipts or fund-raising projects.
4. Limitations should be put on the amount of money allocated to sport clubs other than those imposed by the budget set by the institution.
5. Administrative staff responsible for sport clubs should have control and responsibility over preparation and allocation of funds for sport clubs, but students should determine how the club expends its funds.

As sport clubs organize, develop, and grow, administrative problems tend to accompany this growth. Specifically, sport club financing seems to create most of the problems for educators, administrators, and club members. As a result, different financial practices concerning sport clubs are developed depending on institutional administrative organization and philosophy. Stewart (1978) illustrates this point by stating:

> A continuum illustrating the financial support of sport clubs within institutions of higher education would begin with no support and end with virtual total support. Between the extremes are many variations of financial support. Variations occur not only with the funding source but also with the administration of funds, the structure of the budget, and the allocation of budgets.

Because developing a budget process and finding revenue seem to make up most of the financial problems, the following information concentrates on a successful budget process and will suggest sources of revenue.

THE BUDGET PROCESS

Although there are different funding practices within different institutions, it is necessary for most clubs receiving funds to work through a budget process. This can be a valuable educational experience for sport club members and advisors.

Generally, the budget process consists of four stages: preparation, review and approval, execution, and special budget adjustments. For many sport club programs, this process can occur any time during the year depending on departmental or student government policies.

Budget Preparation

Sport clubs that wish to have their operation subsidized should develop an organized budget request. This budget request is usually submitted to a sport club council or departmental director for an initial review. This process includes covering proper budget procedures and format.

1. *Procedure*
   Each club requesting funding should submit copies of its budget request to the sport club council or departmental director well in advance of scheduled budget hearings. Failure to do this may result in the request being tabled or even rejected for improper procedures. Club representatives should bring enough copies of the budget request for everyone involved in the budget hearings to have a copy. The sport club council or other reviewing body will usually not consider a request unless it is in the proper format. It is conceivable that changes in individual budgets will occur as the bud-

Table 1
Cover Sheet

The Sport Club
Budget and Allocation Request
1984-85

PRESIDENT

FACULTY ADVISOR

DATE CLUB VOTED ON BUDGET

---

get is reviewed by different program administrators and committees.

2. *Format*

A suggested budget format for sport clubs to use in preparing their request includes the following: cover sheet, budget request, current and estimated income and expense statement, current approved budget statement, club balance sheet, list of club officers, and any justification statements the club feels may be necessary to the presentation of the budget plan. The following examples are provided:

a. *Cover Sheet*

The cover sheet (Table 1) should include the name of the club, its purpose, the year during which the information contained in the budget plan will be current, the signature of the president and faculty advisor, and the date the request was approved by the club.

b. *Budget Request*

The budget request (Table 2) is the budget that the club will follow during the next fiscal year (July 1 to June 30) and includes projected income, projected expenses, and the allocation.

(1) *Income*

Income is a list of all the revenues that a club will realize dur-

Table 2
Sport Club Budget Request

Line Item	Amount	
Income:		
Dues: 45 @ $5.00/quarter	$675.00	
Fund-raiser	150.00	
Donations	35.00	
Party	60.00	
Other	15.00	
Total income		$ 935.00
Expenses: Operating		
Phone—local	$110.00	
toll	35.00	
Postage	15.00	
Printing	40.00	
Office supplies	35.00	
Dues—national	100.00	
regional	50.00	
Publicity	160.00	
Party (cross matched)	60.00	
Mileage	402.00	
Food (see breakdown)	390.00	
Lodging	387.00	
Expenses: Capital		
1 bicycle	150.00	
3 rackets	75.00	
Total expenses:		$2,009.00
Less total income		−935.00
Request:		1,074.00

ing its operations. Income includes dues, donations, fund-raisers, and other income. Professional fees for instruction and income for social events should be itemized to show cross matching with expenditures. A minimum dues payment per term per person should be stated.

(2) *Expenses*
Expenses is a list of all the expenditures that a club will realize during its operations. Expenses can be divided into operating and capital expenses.

(3) *Operating Expenses*
Operating expenses are those which will benefit the club for a period of less than three years. Telephone, office supplies,

Table 3
Sport Club Budget Request: Travel Breakdown

Travel	Mileage	Meals	Lodging
Fall:			
Mason City, IA—tournament			
5 people, 2 days, 1 night			
120 mi. × 0.10 × 1 car	$ 12.00		
5 × $5 × 2		$ 50.00	
5 × $7 × 1			$ 35.00
Winter:			
Omaha, NE—tournament			
8 people, 2 days, 2 nights			
380 mi. × 0.09 × 2	$ 68.40		
8 × $4 × 2		$ 64.00	
8 × $6 × 2			$ 96.00
Chicago, IL—qualifying			
12 people, 3 days, 2 nights			
760 mi. × 0.16 × 1 van	$121.60		
12 × $5 × 3		$180.00	
12 × $6 × 2			$ 144.00
Spring:			
Kansas City, MO—nationals			
8 people, 3 days, 2 nights			
1,000 mi. × 0.10 × 2	$200.00		
8 × $4 × 3		$ 96.00	
8 × $7 × 2			$ 112.00
Totals:	$402.00	$390.00	$ 387.00
Total travel:			$1,179.00

Note: The maximum amounts for travel were not used to allow for more people to attend and to hold down our request. We as a club feel that we can get by with the decreased figures.

national dues, postage, insurance, printing, mileage, food, and lodging are all operating expenses. Professional fees for instruction and social events are to be entered here if they are cross matched.

(4) *Capital Expenses*
Capital expenses are those which will benefit the club for a period longer than three years. Equipment purchases are the only capital expenses sport clubs usually have.

(5) *Request*
The difference between the projected expenses and the projected revenues of the club is the allocation request.

Table 4
Sport Club Current and Estimated Income and Expense Statement

Line Item	Actual 7/1-12/31	Estimated 1/1-6/30	Estimated June 30	Budgeted
Income:				
Dues	$315.00	$360.00	$ 675.00	$ 675.00
Fund-raiser	75.00	25.00	100.00	100.00
Donations	0.00	30.00	30.00	30.00
Party	0.00	50.00	50.00	50.00
Other (includes allocation)	241.84	468.66	710.50	710.50
Total income:			$1,565.50	$1,565.50
Expenses: Operating				
Phone—local	$ 50.00	$ 50.00	$ 100.00	$ 100.00
toll	10.00	15.00	25.00	25.00
Postage	7.00	8.00	15.00	15.00
Printing	12.90	37.10	50.00	50.00
Office supplies	25.00	15.00	40.00	40.00
Dues—national	75.00	0.00	75.00	75.00
regional	50.00	0.00	50.00	50.00
Publicity	75.00	35.00	110.00	110.00
Party	0.00	50.00	50.00	50.00
Mileage	87.50	246.00	333.50	333.50
Food	155.00	246.00	401.00	401.00
Lodging	70.00	246.00	316.00	316.00
Expenses: Capital (none were budgeted)	0.00	0.00	0.00	0.00
Total expenses:			$1,565.50	$1,565.50
Net income:			0.00	0.00
Plus funds remaining from last year			90.00	90.00

(6) *Travel and Competition Breakdown*

All travel for which funding is requested (Table 3) must be broken down into its component parts of mileage, food, and lodging. The breakdown must include the destination, the number of miles, the number of people going, and the number of days and nights they will be gone.

This breakdown of travel and competition must be included with both the budget request and the current approved budget.

c. *Current and Estimated Income and Expense Statement (CEIES)*

The CEIES (Table 4) indicates how much of the budget items

Table 5
Sport Club Approved Current Operating Budget

Item	Amount	
Income:		
Dues: 45 @ $5.00	$675.00	
Fund-raiser	100.00	
Donations	30.00	
Party	50.00	
Other	15.00	
GSB allocation	695.50	
Total income		$1,565.50
Expenses:		
Phone—local	$100.00	
toll	25.00	
Postage	15.00	
Printing	50.00	
Office supplies	40.00	
Dues—national	75.00	
regional	50.00	
Publicity	110.00	
Party (cross matched)	50.00	
Mileage	333.50	
Food	401.00	
Lodging	316.00	
Capital equipment	0.00	
Total expenses:		$1,565.50

a club has used for operations to date and how much the club expects to spend during the remainder of the year. All line items on a club's CEIES should also appear on the approved budget.

- Column 1: This is a list by budget line item of all the income and expenses a club has incurred from July 1 to December 1 of the current fiscal year.
- Column 2: This is a list of the income and expenses the club expects to incur from January 1 to June 30 of the current fiscal year.
- Column 3: This should be the sum of each line item in columns 1 and 2.
- Column 4: This is a copy by budget line item of the approved budget.
- Net Income: This is the difference between the total expenses and total income for column 3.

Table 6
Current Travel Breakdown for This Year

Travel	Mileage	Meals	Lodging
Fall:			
Des Moines, IA—tournament			
15 people, 1 day			
65 mi. × 0.10 × 3 cars	$ 19.50		
15 × $5 × 1		$ 75.00	
Dubuque, IA—tournament			
10 people, 2 days, 1 night			
425 mi. × 0.16 × 1 van	$ 68.00		
10 × $4 × 2		$ 80.00	
10 × $7 × 1			$ 70.00
Winter:			
Columbia, MO—qualifying			
15 people, 2 days, 2 nights			
600 mi. × 0.16 × 1 van	$ 96.00		
600 mi. × 0.10 × 1 car	$ 60.00		
15 × $5 × 2		$150.00	
15 × $5 × 2			$150.00
Spring:			
Lincoln, NE—nationals			
8 people, 3 days, 2 nights			
450 mi. × 0.10 × 2 nights	$ 90.00		
8 × $4 × 3		$ 96.00	
8 × $6 × 2			$ 96.00
Totals:	$333.50	$401.00	$316.00
Total travel:			$1,050.50

d. *Current Approved Budget*

Each sport club received an allocation based on an approved budget (Tables 5 and 6) for the current year. A copy of this approved budget must be included with the request for next year's budget by each sport club.

e. *Balance Sheet*

All sport clubs should include a balance sheet (Table 7) for the previous June 30 and an estimated balance sheet for June 30 of the current fiscal year. A list of assets (equipment owned and cash on hand) will normally comprise a club's balance sheet.

(1) *Cash*

The cash balance on the monthly accounting report for the

Table 7
Sport Club Balance Sheet

Assets	Previous June 30	Fiscal June 30
Cash	$ 90.00	$ 90.00
Equipment		
Bicycle	$150.00	$150.00
Stopwatch	$ 22.00	$ 22.00
Net	$ 75.00	$ 75.00
Racquets 5 @ $25.00	$125.00	$125.00
Total assets	$462.00	$462.00
Liabilities—none		

Note: The two columns do not have to be the same. The club in this year did not plan to buy any capital equipment.

previous June 30 must be entered. This cash balance plus the net income from current operations (CEIES net income, column 3) will equal the cash balance for June 30 of the current year.

(2) *Equipment*
A list of all equipment owned by the club comprises the equipment entry of the balance sheet. All equipment should be entered at cost unless it is being depreciated, in which case an entry for the repairs and replacement account should be made.

(3) *Repair and Replacement (R&R)*
The R&R account takes the depreciation, misuse, and breakage of equipment into consideration. Funds in this account are from user fees. The entry on the balance sheet must include the account number, the balance on the previous June 30, and the expected balance on June 30 of the current year.

(4) *Liabilities*
No sport club should have outstanding debts. If the club has ordered a piece of equipment and has not yet been billed, then an entry would be made under liabilities.

(5) *Projected Capital Expenditures*
The club should project the club's capital equipment needs for a period of three years (Table 8). The club should specify all needs and, if possible, give approximate prices.

Table 8
Projected Capital Expenditures

1982-83	None
1983-84	1 net @ $30
1984-85	None

Table 9
Club Officers

Officer Name	Phone #	Address
President: _____	_/_____	_/_____
Vice president: _____	_/_____	_/_____
Treasurer: _____	_/_____	_/_____
Secretary: _____	_/_____	_/_____
Sport club council rep. _____	_/_____	_/_____
Faculty advisor: _____	_/_____	_/_____
Others: _____	_/_____	_/_____

f. *Club Officers*

The sport club council should require that each club list its current officers so that the sport club council treasurer will know who to contact in case of budget complications or errors (Table 9).

g. *Justification Statements*

Club representatives must be thoroughly familiar with their proposed budget, including each item and the justification for it. It is helpful to present a brief written explanation of club goals, past successes, new directions, and general positive aspects concerning the club.

Budget Review and Approval

In summary, the prepared budget is analyzed and approved as it travels through various stages of the review process. This process varies in different institutions. In general, one process involves primarily student government control and another process mainly administrative control.

1. *Student Review Process*
   a. The sport club develops a budget.
   b. The sport club student council reviews the budget.
   c. The student government committee reviews the budget in terms of following proper criteria.
   d. The budget is submitted by the sport club council and finance committee to the government or student body senate. The senate votes to fund the sport club allocation request.
   e. A committee consisting of administrators and students may be included as the last step in the review process to ensure that the budget follows proper institutional fiscal policies and guidelines.

2. *Administrative Control Process*
   a. The sport club develops a budget utilizing departmental budget request forms.
   b. Each club budget is analyzed by a director.
   c. Funds are distributed to clubs on criteria established by the director.
   d. A final budget plan is filed with the director for the year. The sport club council or other student advisory group may be involved in this process with the director.

Budget Execution

Once the budget has been finally modified and adopted, it is essential that it be carefully followed as a club fiscal plan. Many sport club programs have been known to ignore proper budgetary control measures. Therefore, it is essential that clubs have written fiscal and managerial guides to assist them in effective budgetary control. This guide could include the following sections:

1. The office providing financial services for sport clubs. This office provides all forms necessary for conducting club financial transactions such as deposit slips, receipt books, vouchers, purchase orders, ledger pages, and so forth. Monthly computer statements that list all income and expenses may be available to club treasurers.
2. The regular allocation request procedures and format.
3. Periodical financial report procedure and format.
4. Special allocation request procedures and format.
5. Institution services and facilities available for clubs.
6. Organization advisor requirements and responsibilities.

Table 10
Canoe Club Budget Adjustment Request

Item	Amount Budgeted	Amount Used Fall	Change	Proposed Budget
From:				
Fall Travel				
Des Moines River	$ 16.80	0.00	16.80	0.00
Yellow River	$314.40	0.00	254.90	59.50
Upper Iowa River	$289.20	184.65	27.30	77.25
			$299.00	
To:				
Printing and advertising	$ 4.00	0.00	14.00	18.00
Portage pads	$ 0.00	0.00	130.00	130.00
Upper Iowa River (food) (20 people, 3 days)	$113.30	0.00	40.00	153.30
Used Duluth pack (1)	$ 0.00	0.00	15.00	15.00
White River (North Fork) 24 people, 4 days, 1300 miles, equipment rental	$ 50.00	0.00	100.00	150.00
			$299.00	

Explanation:

Because of an unfortunate lack of interest in fall canoeing, the Canoe Club found itself with an excess amount of budgeted funds. We are asking for an adjustment of $299.00 in our budget. Reasons for this reallocation are as follows:

Printing and advertising was budgeted for $4.00. To this date, we have spent $13.29 on printing. Our plans for more flyers make it necessary to budget this added money toward printing and advertising.

The Canoe Club has six canoes, but only one set of portage pads. We would like to purchase five more sets of pads for the rest of our canoes. Portage pads are necessary for our annual trip to the Boundary Waters, and come in handy on our river trips for portaging around fallen trees and transportation to and from vehicles.

For this year's budget, the food for the spring trip to the Upper Iowa River was cut $67.30. We would like to add $40.00 to the food budget for this trip. It will not bring the total to the original value, but will allow for a greater attendance at a reduced cost to the participants.

Campus Recreation is having a sale on used equipment. Their sale includes Duluth packs. The cost of a new pack is $34.00. If the Canoe Club could pick up a used one for $15.00, we would save $19.00. Our present number of two packs are far too few to carry food, tents, and cooking equipment for twenty-four people, our expected attendance for the spring trip.

The Canoe Club's six canoes will accommodate 12 people. On our spring trip we expect 24 participants to attend the trip. As a result, we will need to rent six canoes and a trailer, which will cost approximately one hundred dollars ($100.00). The rental of two GSB vans for the trip is expected to be about $416.00 (1300 miles, $.16/mile, 2 vans). A conservative estimate for food cost is $350.00, bringing the total to $870.00. The Canoe Club would like to keep its outings at a relatively low cost for its participants, who still pay the largest share
(Cont.)

Table 10   (Cont.)
of the cost for the trip. To do this, Canoe Club would like to request that the reallocation
be put toward equipment rental for this trip.

The Canoe Club feels that this reallocation is justified because we are requesting money
that we would have normally spent during fall quarter. Another reason is the promising
outlook for spring quarter. At our meeting last quarter, we had 28 people attending. We
also had twelve more inquires about the club this quarter. With that kind of participation
the club feels it should do its best for its members.

TREASURER	DATE
SFC ADVISOR	DATE
SFC CHAIRMAN	DATE

Special Budget Adjustments

Sport clubs are required to follow their approved budgets once funds
have been allocated for the club's operation. However, provisions may
be made for clubs that find themselves with a necessary unbudgeted expenditure or have made inaccurate estimates regarding expenses or income. This provision is called a budget adjustment and should be used
only when no additional funds are needed. The procedure followed
should be the same procedure that was utilized for the regular allocation
request. The format should consist of three major parts:

1. The budget line items to be reduced (to act as a source of funds).
2. The budget line items to be increased (to act as a use of funds and
   which should equal the sources).
3. An explanation for the change (see example in Table 10).

SOURCES OF INCOME

For most sport clubs the financial burden of providing operating funds
is on the club members. Many clubs are required to raise funds covering
50% or more of their expenses. Therefore, additional sources of income
besides dues and departmental or regular student fee allocation must be
found.

Palmateer (1979) stresses successful fund-raising as follows:

The organization attempting to raise funds can increase its

chances for success by centering the fund-raising activity around some specific event or goal. This personalization of the purpose of the club can be tied in with a Parents' Weekend activity, wine and cheese party, etc. Financially, no matter how well a club plans an initial fund-raising campaign, without good record keeping, future efforts will not come close to realizing their full potential.

Tuveson (1980) emphasizes coordination with university development offices, alumni offices, plus other administrative offices on campus, to help attract additional funds for sport clubs. If special sport club accounts are developed with such offices, club sport participants and club alumni are able to make donations earmarked for the club of their choice.

It is necessary for sport club members to understand basic principles of budgeting such as:

1. Ensuring that services are available to all within the sport club and campus community.
2. Providing programs at the lowest possible cost.
3. Keeping accurate records to indicate costs, types of services, and use of services.
4. Re-evaluating revenue sources each year.
5. Developing long-range plans, not just trying to operate on a day-to-day basis.
6. Understanding the budget preparation techniques of the institution.
7. Being able to justify expenditures.
8. Following the budget as approved and making needed adjustments as allowed.
9. Estimating budget expenditures and revenue carefully.
10. Presenting a convincing, realistic budget request.

However, cooperation is an essential ingredient in the sport club financing process. Usually, for a club to develop and thrive, the members must be active and willing to work with the various administrative personnel, student leaders, committee members, and different campus organizations, departments, and offices. Very few club programs are funded without a cooperative approach by sport club members.

Acknowledgment

This chapter was originally published in *Theoretical and operational aspects of intramural sports* (pp. 288-302) edited by T.P. Sattler, P.J. Graham, and D.C. Baily, 1978, West Point, NY: Leisure Press. Copyright by NIRSA. Reprinted by permission.

REFERENCES

Mueller, C.E., & Reznik, J.W. (1979). *Intramural-recreational sports* (5th ed.). New York: John Wiley.

Palmateer, D. (1979). The dollars and sense approach to sport club funding. *Journal of Physical Education and Recreation, 50*(3), 46-67.

Phelps, D.E. (1970). *Current practices and recommended guidelines for the administration of sports clubs in selected four-year midwest colleges and universities.* Unpublished doctoral dissertation, Indiana University, Bloomington.

Sliger, I.T. (1978). *Sports club survey.* Unpublished internal report, University of Tennessee.

Stewart, S.L. (1978). Sports clubs and financing. In T.P. Sattler, P.J. Graham, & D.C. Bailey (Eds.), *Theoretical and operational aspects of intramural sports* (pp. 303-305). West Point: Leisure Press.

Tuveson, A. (1980). Club sports' fund-raising alternatives. *NIRSA Journal, 4*(2), 18-20.

CHAPTER 12

The Citadel's Operational Guidelines Criteria for the Allocation of Sport Club Council Funds

1. The purpose of this statement is to ensure that all member clubs receive equitable treatment in the allocation of Council funds on the basis of standards approved by them. To this end, the Council herein established (1) procedures to be followed by clubs in requesting funds, and by the Council in determining allocations and (2) criteria on which the Council's decisions are to be based. Procedures are intended to ensure complete exchange of all relevant information among clubs in an orderly fashion. Criteria are supplied, not only for fairness, but also for assisting clubs in preparing and organizing their proposals for allocations, and for expediting the Council's decision making.
2. Council funds shall be available only to clubs holding membership on the Council.
3. Procedures
   a. Each club will prepare a typewritten proposal to include budgets and their explanation and justification as detailed in the criteria. This information should be as complete as possible. The Council will establish both a deadline for submitting proposals, and penalties, if any, for failure to meet this deadline.
   b. The Council will review all proposals in terms of criteria. Any relevant records should be available to the Council at this time. If the members of the Council have any questions about a club's proposal, or feel some information is lacking (explanation, elaboration, justification, etc.), such points shall be made available

to the club as soon as possible and before the club's oral presentation to the Council.

   c. Arrangements shall be made (date, time, place) for each club requesting funds to make a brief oral presentation of its position to the assembled Council, and to respond to the Council's questions about the proposal.

   d. Meeting as a whole, the Council will do the following:

     (1) Determine each club's justified needs in the light of all criteria, including those concerning the club's responsibilities to the Council. In other words, penalties or rewards, if any, should be made by respectively decreasing or increasing its justified need.

     (2) Determine each club's allocation based on justified needs in relation to the total monies available and the justified needs of the other clubs eligible to receive funds.

     (3) Submit proposed budgets to the Vice President for Administration and Finance for approval.

3. Criteria

   a. Criteria are divided into those concerning budgets, the explanation and justification of budgets, and the performance of a club's duties as a Council member. Proposals should be written and reviewed on this basis.

   b. Budgets

     (1) In its proposal, each club will include budgets for the previous and current years and a proposed budget for the coming year, including funds requested from the Council.

     (2) Budgets should be accurate numerical summaries of all of a club's expenses versus all its revenues, together with their balance. Revenues may range from dues and gate receipts to gifts and projects. Expenses can be broken down generally into instruction, equipment, facilities, officials, travel, special programs, and membership fees. Budgets should be itemized to the extent that the nature of all incomes and expenditures is clear.

     (3) Proposed needs should be estimated as accurately as possible based on a club's plans and justifiable expenses and its revenue. No attempt should be made to underestimate or exaggerate requests.

   c. Explanation and justification of budgets.

     (1) These areas should constitute the main body of a club's proposal and should be the initial area of consideration by the Council, keeping in mind at all times the goals of the Council and of the club involved.

     (2) Instruction: Amount paid for instruction should reflect the needs of the club and the time and expertise of the coach.

(3) Equipment
  a. Equipment shall be limited to that which is permanently retained by the club and which is used only during club activities. Such equipment shall be college property. It should not include personal items that are used exclusively by one individual.
  b. Uniforms that are required for play are retained by the club on a year to year basis and may be justifiable expenses, as may the maintenance of such items.
  c. Purchases should be considered in relation to the club's current inventory and its necessary maintenance and/or replacement.

(4) Facilities
  a. A detailed explanation of all facility charges should be included.
  b. Suitable facilities under the control of the Intramural Department must be used when available.

(5) Officials
  a. Officials needed should be detailed, including the number of officials per match, the number of matches, and the cost per official per match.
  b. Where a certified official is absolutely essential, payment will not exceed the specified minimum amount for that sport.
  c. Payment for noncertified officials shall be consistent with the scale established by the IM Department.

5. Travel
  a. A travel plan shall be filed with the Chair of the Sport Club Council specifically indicating destination, time of departure, mode of transportation, time of return, lodging place (if an overnight stay is necessary), emergency phone number, and any individual departure from the club's travel plan. This information must be submitted before travel funds are approved. (See Form 1.)
  b. All travel must be carefully justified and should take into consideration whether the same competition or quality of program is available at a lower cost.
  c. Clubs should attempt to combine matches or programs in one geographical area into a single trip.
  d. Support should be given only for the minimum number of players or participants needed. Having a number of substitutes is justifiable.
  e. Meals and lodging are justifiable expenses at the rate of $16.00 and $40.00 daily, respectively.
  f. Expenses for travel should never exceed the amount specified for college business.

Form 1
Travel Plan

Name of club _____

Destination _____

Date and time of departure _____

Date and time of return to the Citadel _____

Lodging place (if overnight) _____

Emergency phone numbers _____

Individual _____

Deviations from club's plan _____

_____

_____

_____

_____

_____

_____
Signature of Coach or Club Advisor

    g. Where competition is on a dual basis, there should be approximately the same amount of home events as away events.

    h. Where competition is on a multiple team basis in a single location, the college should host its share of events.

    i. Only qualified persons should be funded to go to national or major events.

6. Special programs
    a. Funding for special programs such as workshops or master classes is a justifiable expense when serving a majority of the club's membership and/or the college community.
    b. Local resources should be used when qualified and available.

7. Membership and/or entry fees
    a. Team membership and team entry fees are a justifiable expense when required to obtain competition or certification.
    b. Individual memberships are not justifiable expenses.
    c. Individual entry and/or membership fees may be a justifiable

expense when the individual is participating as an official representative of the club.

8. Income
   a. A club is encouraged to consider fund-raising activities in the preparation of its budget.
   b. The Council is more likely to favor a club's request if it indicates the club's desire and/or willingness to cover some of the club's expense.
   c. Fund-raising events that may be included are:
      (1) Those undertaken in previous or current years.
      (2) Anticipated activities related to the club and depended upon by the college community.
   d. Dues should be included when established by the club and using a reasonable projection of membership.
   e. Solicitation as fund-raising must be coordinated through and approved by the Vice President for Development.

9. Special events
   a. All clubs are strongly encouraged to host at least one event annually (more if possible) that is open to and participated in by the college community. This could include tournaments, exhibitions, workshops, and other events but not regular competitive events.

PART IV

Liability Concerns of Sport Clubs

T wo essential liability concerns can drastically affect campus recreation directors as well as club supervisors, advisors, coaches, and club members: (a) failure to provide proper instruction and (b) failure to warn participants of potential risks. Within the past two decades, the failure to properly instruct or coach has been grounds for many negligence suits, mainly in contact sport activities.

The courts have been very explicit in citing coaches and teachers on such matters as failure to communicate the medical, scientific, and statistical knowledge relative to participation in sport activities; negligence in or failure to make information regarding inherent risks available to both players and parents; and failure to establish a responsible office or person to gather and distribute the information about risk to the participants. Also, clubs can be found to be at fault when they do not publish policies that stress safety in instruction.

One topic of great concern that has been discussed for a number of years is insurance coverage for sport club participants. Insurance should cover not only the costs of injury repair and recovery but also the incurrence of liability. For example, one coverage plan provided essentially for high schools, called the Student Protection Trust (from the Ruedlinger Companies of Topeka, KS), offers "medical and rehabilitation expenses, transportation costs, costs for remodeling the family home to accommodate the injured and wages lost by parents who have to miss work to help administer care to the injured athlete." Insurance plans should be investigated by sport club administrators with the ultimate goal of complete protection for members and sponsors alike.

These concerns and many others are discussed in this section. In "Problems of Liability in Campus Recreation Sport Club Programs," Rankin and Fraki address the matters of the validity of release forms, liability for nonuniversity property and equipment, and staff liability. They stress that no one can predict the outcome of any individual case. Therefore, we should be prudent in our administration of sport clubs, but we should not become unduly alarmed and frightened into inactivity.

The second article is a composite of several approaches to the question of liability. Collaborators Hirt, Ludwig, Capra, and Fletcher address the subjects of university legal officers and administration, purchasing departments, claims managers, trainers and physicians at contests, release forms, injury report forms, facility safety management, and travel practices.

CHAPTER 13

Current Problems of Liability in Campus Recreation Sport Club Programs

Janna S. Rankin
Arthur N. Fraki
Temple University

A number of issues are related to the problem of liability for injuries in campus recreation programs, including sport clubs. Before these specific issues are dealt with, however, a few general observations should be made.

First, liability for personal injuries (tort liability) is largely based upon common law principles. The common law is the result of hundreds of years of judicial experience and the commonsense observations of the manner in which the ordinary people behave as they go about the routines of their daily lives. The key to an understanding of common law is an appreciation of a mythical figure known as "the reasonably prudent person." By and large, an individual's liability for injuries to another will be determined on the basis of whether he or she acted as a "reasonably prudent person" under the circumstances. If an individual is a trained professional in campus recreation, then the liability issue may usually be phrased in this way: Did the defendant act in a manner consistent with the reasonable standards of the profession, considering all of the facts available to her or him at the time of the injury in question?

One can readily see that many issues of liability may be resolved with no reference to any technical or illogical peculiarities of law but will largely be determined on the basis of the knowledge possessed by both professional recreators and mature adults.

There really is no special body of law or precedent (the record of prior cases that helps shape current approaches to law), for campus recreation departments. There is a growing body of case law concerning sports and recreation, but on the whole speculation about what might happen in a particular campus recreation situation must depend upon general experience in tort law. Also, as a universal caution, statutes and judicial decisions in each state may serve to modify the general principles.

THE VALIDITY OF RELEASE FORMS

Under the age of majority (18 years in most jurisdictions today), a contractual release from liability is unlikely to be effective in insulating a sport club program or an institution from liability. Neither may a parent or guardian release liability for their child or ward. On the other hand, because many states now permit lawsuits between parent and child, it is possible that if a parent gives permission for participation in an activity that the parent knows to be beyond the ability of the child, the parent may have to contribute to the amount the injured child may recover against the campus recreation activity. That was the result in a significant California case in which a teenage boy was seriously injured in a motorcycle race. The California Supreme Court held that if the race promoter could show that the parents knew or should have realized that the race was too dangerous or beyond their son's capacity, the parents could be held to pay part of the damages (*American Motorcycle Association v. Superior Court*, 1978).

With regard to adults, and most college students are considered legally adults today, the law has been somewhat mixed. On the one hand, courts are very suspicious of agreements that excuse negligent conduct. Releases are likely to be considered contracts of adhesion; that is, because they are prepared by an agency or organization with superior knowledge and power, all that the would-be participant can do is agree (or adhere) to the dictated terms or forego the activity. Because most persons reject the notion that they are likely to be crippled, killed, or seriously injured in a recreational activity, they are likely to sign virtually any release form, no matter how broadly worded it is. Recognizing all this, courts have a tendency to either construe or interpret releases very narrowly or to reject them altogether and declare them void as against public policy. The broader the release and the more vague its terms, the more likely it is to be rejected or interpreted in favor of the injured participant. Particularly if a release attempts to insulate an agency from liability for "negligent" or "grossly negligent" behavior, courts may adopt the attitude that it is against public policy to sanction dangerous or unlawful behavior. For a specific example, see *Rosen v. LTV Recreational Development, Inc.* (1978), in which a general release signed by an experienced skier when he purchased his season pass was held invalid when applied to an injury the skier suffered when he collided with a steel signpost that was negligently placed in the middle of a ski slope.

In contrast, some decisions have held that, because recreation has not been considered one of life's necessities, a properly presented and executed release form should be considered to demonstrate a voluntary acceptance of foreseeable hazards. In other words, unlike releases attached to landlord-tenant leases or employment contracts, because no one is forced by necessity to engage in recreational activities, voluntary releases should be honored. Thus, when a woman who signed a general release for negligence as a precondition for joining a health club fell on a slippery pool deck, a New York court dismissed her suit, characterizing her as a "volunteer" (*Ciofalo v. Vic Tanny Gyms, Inc.*, 1961). It should be noted, however, that the New York legislature was so troubled by the results in this case that it enacted a statute voiding any agreement eliminating liability for negligence in fee-based recreational activities (N.Y. General Obligations Law S5-326, 1963).

Despite the problems of reliance on release forms that we have detailed, there are still a number of good reasons why an appropriately designed information or activities form should be required of participants in sport club activities, signed by participants if they are of legal age in your state or by participants and their parents if they are younger. (Parents may sign a general permission form when their child goes off to college, or parental premission for oncampus activities may be implied.)

First, an appropriate form should set forth a reasonably detailed description of the activity, including the level of skill required for participation and any particular risks of injury not readily apparent from the program description itself. This form should also list clothing and equipment to be furnished by the participant as well as that to be provided by the organizer or program. The form should require certification by the participants that they are physically capable of undertaking the activity. It should provide a place for listing any physical or other conditions that might effect the ability of the participant to successfully undertake the activity or might be crucial in case of injury (such as intolerance to certain drugs or allergies to bee stings.)

If the activity is particularly demanding or the participant has a condition that raises doubt as to his or her participation, a physician's certification may be required, although this would be relatively rare.

Finally, one copy of the signed form should be returned to the campus recreation office before the activity is undertaken, and another should be retained by the participant. This procedure will ensure that the participant was actually aware of the contents of the form, which should be legible and not buried on the back of some other document.

A form such as Sample Form 1 largely eliminates the possibility that an injured participant can claim that the activity sponsor was negligent in not informing him or her of the risks involved in an activity. It also

Sample Form 1
Central College Recreation Association
Activity Participation Form

Activity Description: Blue Mountain Backpacking Trip

This is a 15-mile hike on the Blue Mountain Trail from the trailhead to Blue Lake (seven miles) where we will camp overnight, and out to the highway at Milepost 10. This is a moderately difficult hike that does not require any technical climbing ability, but does put stress on good physical conditioning. There are some steep slippery stretches both uphill and downhill. Weather conditions are usually variable, and the trail may become particularly difficult if there is a rainstorm. Wildlife may appear at any time, and black bear are known to frequent the region. Rattlesnakes are also present in the area.

Equipment required to be furnished by the participant:

a. Well broken-in hiking boots with lug-soles or other antislip shoes.
b. Rain gear, warm sweater, hat, and gloves.
c. Change of clothing appropriate for temperature range from below freezing to 75 °F.
d. Sleeping bag (may be rented from Recreation Association).

Equipment supplied by the Recreation Association:

a. Backpacks (you may, of course, bring your own if you desire).
b. Tents (two-person tents). (You may bring your own if you desire.)
c. Food, beverages, and utensils.
d. First-aid equipment and snake antivenin.

No alcoholic beverages, illegal substances, cigarettes, cigars, or pipes may be brought on this trip. This area is subject to forest fires.

Participant acknowledges that he or she has read and understands the aforementioned information. Participant further certifies that he or she is in good physical condition and is fit to participate in this activity. Participant understands that this is a wilderness recreational activity, that unexpected hazards may arise, and that he or she must always be alert for dangers to self and to other participants.

Signature of participant _____

Date _____

Signature of parent or guardian (if participant is under 18) _____

IMPORTANT!

I have the following physical condition(s) which may affect my ability to successfully participate in this trip or which may be significant in case of emergency or accident. (If none, check here _____)

Date _____   Signed _____

eliminates the problem that sometimes arises when a participant claims that the recreation department was informed of a particular physical injury, allergy, or condition but did nothing about it and was therefore negligent. Although a form such as this does not attempt to insulate a campus recreation agency from liability for active negligence, which would probably be rejected by the courts, it does serve to limit successful claims of negligence to those which reflect actual misfeasance on the part of the organizers or trip leaders. By making participants aware of the hazards and their responsibilities, it is hoped that the use of the form could also cut down on the number of careless injuries.

Probably the only way to totally eliminate negligence suits is to totally eliminate campus sport club activities. No doubt at least some administrators and their lawyers would advocate such a position. Eliminating total programs or limiting them to such extremely low-risk activities as Ping-Pong and square dancing would defeat and destroy the very purposes to which the campus recreation movement is dedicated. The question should be phrased this way: How many injuries that engender liability suits can be limited to an absolute minimum, and what steps should be taken to assure that those intramural participants who are injured are fairly compensated and rehabilitated?

Because of the perceived negative connotations and the professional insult reflected in a finding of negligence and liability, or even in a settlement in which an injured participant receives a substantial amount of money, many recreators tend to focus on the unfairness and unreasonableness of the stigma rather than on the real costs of an injury. For example, in a fictional case, during a footrace at a picnic, one of the participants at the end of the race hurled himself into the adjacent lake, which was clearly signed "No Swimming." He struck his head on a submerged trash barrel and was rendered paraplegic. A court held that the park commission could be found negligent in permitting its trash barrels to be submerged in murky water. The case was settled for hundreds of thousands of dollars. If we focus on which party was "wrong," we might well feel that the injured plaintiff was careless and undeserving and therefore should get nothing. On the other hand, if we concentrate on the injury, it is obvious that unless we are to discard this man and throw his family on welfare, the enormous cost of medical, therapeutic, and rehabilitative care will have to be met by someone.

In a number of areas the law has recognized that old concepts of "fault" are largely outmoded. An employee injured in the course of his job is compensated under worker's compensation insurance without regard to fault, even if his own negligence was the cause of the injury. A participant in a recreational activity injured by a defective product such as a flawed football helmet or a dune buggy that turns over may recover damages from the manufacturer, even if the defect was not readily preventable and the manufacturer was not negligent. In these areas of law, it has been recognized that compensation by those best able to pass the cost along to the public at large is more important than singling out some person or enterprise at "fault."

We have not yet reached this stage in ordinary provision of services or nonemployment injuries. Despite the requirement of fault, the great expense of defending serious lawsuits and the fact that a plaintiff who loses need not generally reimburse a defendant for the costs of defense creates a strong impetus for the insurance company attorneys, who defend most major negligence suits, to attempt to settle for a reasonable figure. This is often done even if judgment for the plaintiff is not nearly merited. Because of all this, recreation professionals must stop assuming that any settlement or loss of damages suit automatically labels them incompetent or unprofessional.

Another complaint generally heard is that the amount of money recovered is exorbitant, making millionaires out of ordinary people. Although there are occasional excessive recoveries, major recoveries of $100,000 and over are by and large limited to serious injuries that engender huge costs.

For example, in one famous ski injury case the quadriplegic plaintiff recovered $1.5 million. Yet at the time of the trial, $70,000 in medical expenses had already accumulated. Projected costs of future medical care, nursing, medications, and hospitalization were over $2.5 million, without considering inflation. (*Sunday v. Stratton Corp.*, 1978.) Anyone who has had a serious illness or had family members who are ill or injured can readily appreciate that $1 million is not an exorbitant amount for the treatment and rehabilitation of a permanently crippled individual. The widespread notion that unscrupulous individuals are recovering hundreds of thousands of dollars for mysterious back ailments is largely a myth.

If one can look realistically at the liability issue and recognize that high costs and lawsuits are not going to go away, one can take steps to minimize both injury and liability. Among these are the following.

- *Resist the temptation to ''make do.''* Many injuries and consequent law suits are engendered by the use of broken, patched, faulty equipment, or by older equipment that doesn't meet the state of the art. This is an area where desire for a full program with maximum participation clashes with professional safety concerns. Because it is extremely unlikely that the eager sport club participant will recognize the need for caution and safety, the recreation professional must do so! Common sense dictates that certain equipment, particularly if it is safety related, must meet highest professional standards. Cracked helmets, splintered bats, protruding bolts, and worn mats all present hazards of injury and liability. A firm ''no'' to the use of such equipment is the best defense to a potential lawsuit.
- *Eliminate those activities which entail high risk with little reward, particularly when there are less dangerous alternatives.* An example of such an activity is ''tray sliding'' as described in a conversation with a Cornell University student. A time-honored tradition of careening down

a snow-covered hill on cafeteria trays was brought to an abrupt end (at least officially) when a participant was paralyzed in a collision. Tradition or not, such a dangerous, unnecessary activity virtually invites injury and liability, particularly because voluntary assumption of risk and contributory negligence have now been modified in most states so that they will only serve to reduce, not eliminate, liability.

Certain recognized sports activities, for example, trampolining, diving, and tackle football, engender a disproportionate share of serious recreational and sports injuries. Advocates of these activities may wax eloquent about their virtues, but campus recreation officials must ask themselves if the experience afforded by such activities is sufficiently distinctive and valuable to justify the increased risk of liability. This analysis, incidently, is a key component of a good risk management program by your institution.

- *Offer insurance policies for trips and hazardous activities.* Insurance cannot eliminate the risk of liability suits because a person's own insurance will not be considered when damages are evaluated, but insurance will provide a financial cushion to absorb the major initial costs of injuries and treatment and may serve to discourage minor nuisance suits and to put injured participants in a more cooperative and positive frame of mind toward the recreation activity. Contrary to public belief, not everyone is litigious.
- *Hire qualified personnel.* Supervisory and instructional personnel should have the required professional certifications where called for, although, in terms of negligence, it is what a person does that is critical, not his or her credentials. Someone who has had first aid and emergency training should always be available. A substantial proportion of lawsuits are engendered not by the accident itself but through a failure to render appropriate treatment. The number of personnel must be adequate to supervise the activity. However, as participants reach higher levels of proficiency the need for continual direct supervision decreases; at the novice or learning stages of an activity, inadequate supervision and instruction are often causes of liability.

Parenthetically, something should be said here about recreational activities in which the participation of the campus recreation agency is minimal; for example, checking out sports equipment, providing a playing field for unsupervised activity, or even just hanging a bulletin board through which individuals interested in activities from skydiving to chess can arrange meetings. If it is clear that there is no official sanction for such activities, liability would be limited to the equipment or facilities under the control of the recreation program (for example, a hidden hole in the playing field, a basketball backboard that breaks because of a missing bolt, or a tennis racquet whose weakened head flies off and hits someone). It is when there is something more than minimal participation but less than full supervision and sponsorship that a campus recreation program might get into difficulties. Recall the Cornell tray-sliding case. The university provided the trays, lit the field or slope, put straw or padding around the trees, and erected a snow fence. Arguably, this was sufficient involvement to make the university responsible for the injuries. Ironically, if it had done little or nothing to make the activity safe and to encourage it, Cornell would probably have escaped liability altogether.

LIABILITY FOR NON-UNIVERSITY PROPERTY AND EQUIPMENT

Where the recreation department merely provides transportation and access to an off-campus activity such as a ski area, amusement park, or ball field, there is little likelihood of liability unless it is proven that the department was negligent in its selection of the particular activity site.

The question of liability for independent non-university-run programs operating on campus or sport clubs as part of the regular recreation program is quite complex, as is the issue of liability for programs conducted by independent contractors, part-time employees, and volunteers.

Considerations here take us into the realm of agency law, master-servant and independent contractor law, nondelegatable duties, and related areas. Following are some basic generalizations, with the caution that this common law area may be modified by statutes and judicial decisions in individual states.

The rule of "respondeat superior," states that the employer is responsible for the tortious or negligent actions of employees when the employee is acting "in the course of his/her employment." Thus, whether a person is a full-time, part-time, or temporary employee, as long as the individual is generally carrying out assigned duties, the university will have liability. This applies if the particular employee has not strayed so far from his or her assigned task that it can be said that the person was no longer engaged in the university's business but was, to use the quaint legal term, on a "frolic or detour" of his or her own. The courts tend to be very liberal in defining "scope of employment," especially if the work is on the road, on some overnight or long-term excursion.

Even if the employee has violated a specific instruction, the university is still likely to be held liable as long as that person is generally functioning in the university's interest.

On the other extreme, a truly independent contractor who supplies materials, sets hours, and relies on professional knowledge with no direct university supervision will insulate a university from liability, unless of course the university has been negligent in the hiring of the contractor

or if that contractor is carrying out an integral, "nondelegatable" duty
of the university.

How does one distinguish between an independent contractor and an
employee or servant? There are no hard-and-fast rules, but there are a
number of criteria:

- Control and direction—the greater the university's control over the
  methods and manner of work, the more likely it is to be an employment situation.
- Materials and tools—if the university's own equipment is utilized in
  the activity, that is an indication of employment.
- Skill—the greater the degree of professional skill, the more likely the
  person is to be considered an independent contractor.
- Method of payment—a contract for a lump sum, or better yet a rental
  of facilities with the outside individual charging and keeping fees for
  the activity would be an indication of an independent contractor.
- The nature of the business—an independent business with its own
  structure, different customers, and independent economic viability,
  and work being done that is an activity which is not an integral part
  of university services.

Following are some hypothetical examples. Suppose that Central
University wishes to offer a program of instructional tennis and intramural
competition. It contracts with Pro Sports Incorporated, which leases the
university's tennis courts for a flat hourly fee. Pro Sports provides its own
trained professional instructors. It also provides balls, racquets, and training aids and charges each student-participant a fee for instruction and
participation. Pro Sports is a corporation that offers similar services to
other schools and municipalities.

This is an independent contractor situation, and assuming that the
choice of contractor is a reasonable one and that injuries do not arise from
flaws in university property, it is very likely that the university will escape liability in case of injury. Nevertheless, because courts are reluctant
to leave an injured person with no recourse, it should be standard practice to require that contractors possess substantial, paid-up liability insurance, and agree to indemnify the university for all litigation and
damages and hold the university harmless in case a participant is injured.

Suppose that instead of using Pro Sports Incorporated, the university
hires a graduate student who is a tennis pro to run its sport club program on a part-time basis. The university pays a seasonal salary, supplies equipment, and collects fees for the program. This would likely be
regarded as an employer-employee situation (master-servant), and the
university would be liable for injuries resulting from negligence.

The use of student or community volunteers to drive vehicles or
supervise programs will usually result in a liability situation in case of

participant injury, whether a court interprets the situation as a "joint venture," part-time employment, or voluntary master-servant relationship. Even if a student used his or her own car to drive a group to a university-sponsored activity with no compensation, many courts will strain to find ultimate responsibility with the university.

In another typical case, a teacher who was in charge of a tennis program at a junior college authorized a student to act for him in driving other participants in the program. The student was permitted to fill his tank at the college's gas pump. When the overloaded car's brakes failed, the school was held liable for its negligent failure to provide safe transportation (*Hanson v. Reedley Joint Union High School District*, 1941). A more recent Delaware case reached the same conclusion from similar facts (*Adams v. Kline*, 1968). By contrast, when a school district contracted with a licensed transportation company to take students to a state basketball tournament, there was no liability for injuries from a bus accident because the school merely designated the time and place of departure and return (*Lify v. Joint School District*, 1969). Again there is the irony that the more active the university is to ensure a safe, quality recreational experience, the more likely it is to be liable should someone be injured. The question is whether you desire students to be involved in relatively safe, constructive recreational activities with some risk of liability or would rather leave them to their own recreational devices with inherently greater risk of injury and antisocial or dangerous conduct.

Sport clubs, which are given even a small amount of university support and recognition in terms of finance, facilities, coaching, or equipment, are likely to be treated as integral to a university's function and should not be viewed as a sure method of avoiding institutional liability. On the other hand, where clubs are completely informal and have no direct university recognition or control, the school will likely escape liability. See, for example, *Davies v. Butler* (1974), where, in an action for wanton misconduct, members of an unincorporated drinking club at the University of Nevada-Reno was held individually liable, but the university itself was not. The drinking activities did not take place on campus.

In the rather typical recreation situation where a group of students goes on a university-sponsored outing in two vans, one driven by a professor and the other by a student with the university paying travel expenses, it is likely that if the student gets into an accident after consuming a couple of beers at dinner, the university will be held liable.

STAFF LIABILITY

There is a widespread misunderstanding that if one is employed by a corporation, agency, or institution, the employer's liability will insulate the employee. This is simply not true. Even in the relatively few places where sovereign or governmental immunity will protect a state insitution from a lawsuit, the employee who is directly responsible for the injury is liable, unless a specific statute prevents liability. There is a Federal Driver's statute that insulates federal employees from liability to vehicle accidents and makes the government liable, and a number of states protect police, firefighters, and occasionally teachers. But on the whole, if you negligently injure someone, you are responsible.

Even where some statutory immunity appears to exist, courts are reluctant to permit the negligent person to escape liability. For example, in a recent Florida case, a student claimed that a teacher ordered him to perform a trampoline exercise that resulted in injury. Despite a state statute apparently relieving teachers from liability when they act within the scope of their employment, the Florida Supreme Court ruled that the teacher could be sued and should be personally liable for the amount of damages above the maximum permitted by the State Tort Claims Act. The court stated, "Holding public employees personally responsible for their own negligence may provide an incentive for more careful performance of official duties and obligations" (*District School Board v. Talmadge*, 1980).

Despite this, the number of cases in which the employee of a university actually winds up paying for his or her defense and for damages is extremely small. Why is this? First, because of respondeat superior, the employer will inevitably be named in the suit as well. Because the university invariably has more money, or a "deeper pocket," the plaintiff's attorney will normally seek to recover against the institution.

Second, all universities have some form of indemnity policy, which agrees to defend and protect university employees who are sued for injuries arising out of their employment. You should be aware of your institution's indemnification policy to see how completely it covers you. Some policies eliminate coverage if the employee has been "grossly or willfully negligent," or is an intentional wrongdoer. Because it is easy for a plaintiff to allege these things, an indemnity policy should provide for an independent review of the employee's actions even if there are such allegations or, indeed, a finding of gross negligence by a jury.

On the whole, a campus recreation professional has little to fear in terms of individual liability from negligence lawsuits. The psychological and emotional costs of involvement are likely to be much more damaging than the financial ones.

Finally, it should be reiterated that no one can predict the outcome of any individual case. Facts, local rules and laws, and judicial whim are all variables. Thus, not only should the generalities in this chapter be taken with caution, but gossip, personal experience, war stories, and other legal horror tales should be treated with a good deal of healthy skepticism. Even reports of exorbitant and outrageous jury verdicts in the press should not be cause for undue alarm. Most outrageous and unwarranted decisions will be modified or reversed by appellate courts in decisions that are rarely publicized.

Acknowledgment

This chapter was originally published in *Intramural-recreational sports: Its theory and practice* (pp. 141-147) edited by L.S. Preo, L. Fabian, W.M. Holsberry, J.W. Reznik, and F. Rokosz, 1982, Corvallis, OR: NIRSA. Copyright by NIRSA. Reprinted by permission.

REFERENCES

Adams v. Kline, 239 A. 2d 230 (e1. 1968).

American Motorcycle Association v. Superior Court, 20 Cal.3d 578, 578 P.2d 899, 146 Cal Rptr. 182 (1978).

Ciofalo v. Vic Tanney Gyms, Inc., 10 N.Y.2d 294, 117 N.E.2d 295, 220 N.Y.S.2d 962 (1961).

Davies v. Butler, 602 P.2d 605 (Nev. 1974).

District School Board v. Talmadge, 381 So.2d 698 (Fla. 1980).

Hanson v. Reedley Joint Union High School District, 43 Cal. App. 2d 643, 111 P.2d 415 (1941).

Lify v. Joint School District, 42 Wes.2d 253, 166 N.W.2d 809 (1969).

N.Y. General Obligations Law S5-326 (1963).

Rosen v. LTV Recreational Development, Inc., 569 F.2d 1117 (10th Cir. 1978).

Sunday v. Stratton Corp., 136 Vt. 293, 390 a.2d 298 (1978).

CHAPTER 14

Insurance/Liability/Risk Management Concerns in Sport Clubs

Sam Hirt
Vanderbilt University

Donald F. Ludwig
University of Southern California

Loretta Capra
Colorado State University

Mark Fletcher
University of Denver

The Sport Club program at Vanderbilt University is included within the Office of Student Affairs and is part of the Campus Recreation Department, which administers 17 active clubs.

All liability and risk management concerns are handled in a multitude of ways. Some methods include the Sport Club booklet, waiver and release forms, CRD literature brochures, review at all coaches' meetings and discussion with visiting coaches, and utilization of the inside legal counseling available.

As programs expand in the 1980s, sport club directors must become familiar with the administrative officers at their institutions who determine the legal policies. These contact persons and procedures to follow will be addressed here.

1. *University Legal Officers and Administration:* Every effort must be made to become familiar with liability and risk management policies at your institution. Also, the administrative officers need to know the sport club program. These individuals can offer invaluable

assistance and advice to improve and protect all parties involved. These methods would include:

- Putting waiver/release forms in writing.
- Ruling on eligibility situations.
- Discussing spectators' rights and responsibilities.
- Giving advice on facility safety to provide a safe premise.
- Reviewing the total university liability coverage and possibly purchasing additional life/accident insurance for the participants.
- Establishing proper channels to approve clubs annually which would adhere to all policies and guidelines.
- Checking out legal issues when using outside and community facilities.
- Facts dictate position and when injury occurs write report immediately.
- Discuss specific injury situations that could occur in every club sport program.

It is always recommended that correct protocol be followed when answers are sought to these legal questions. Establishing a close relationship with legal and administrative officers is vital.

2. *Purchasing Department:* All van and car contracts and rates are reviewed. Proper travel and return forms must be filed in the proper time frame.
3. *Claims Manager in Risk Management Department:* Program administrators should be familiar with the worker's compensation and medical insurance policies and how they interrelate with various participants, such as students, faculty, and staff.
4. *Hospital Locations:* Locations of hospitals in the immediate area and the emergency room procedures should be discussed with sport club coaches. Local doctors' offices and clinics should be stressed in case of emergency care to teams or visitors.
5. *Trainer and Doctors at Contests:* Although often expensive, these are recommended. University trainers work in conjunction with the athletic department, but their services are available. You must make appropriate arrangements for home and away contests.
6. *Staff and Support Personnel:* You should be aware of proper procedures to follow when injury occurs. Your administrators need to be advised of all developments. The coaches, injured party, and officials become involved when filling out proper forms. Expediency is vital because the situation includes dealing with the safety of the participants and the concerns of the parents.

Various techniques and procedures have been developed or are in the process of development involving the following suggestions:

- All legal wording in publications is checked by legal officer.

- Get administrative support of your procedures.
- Install phones and post emergency numbers on or near facilities.
- Have legal officers speak at your coaches' meetings—a question-and-answer period is constructive.
- Examine equipment and facilities frequently. Take plant operations and legal staff to facility areas.
- Invite officials' comments to strengthen your program.
- Notify security department concerning your events for crowd and traffic control.
- Review your legal concerns with the athletic department for insurance and liability concerns.
- Maintain an accident/injury file in your office.

Our main responsibility is for the *safety* of all those involved. The safety factor becomes an oral and written duty every day, and it is subject to review to constantly strengthen your program. Continue to be aggressive in explaining the required rules and regulations that must be followed by all parties. Keep looking for deficiencies and inherent dangers in your facilities and put in writing methods and ways to improve the situation at your school. Everyone must know what personal limits and responsibilities are for liability and risk management as directors and assistants in sport clubs.

FACILITY SAFETY MANAGEMENT

This presentation will address the issue of facility safety management for sport clubs. No matter what type of intramural recreation facility we use (new or old, indoor or outdoor), we, as professionals in the field, must keep our facilities as safe as possible. The following is a brief summary of suggested methods used to keep facilities safe:

1. The most important thing to do is document, in writing, all your observations and requests for repair.
2. At least twice a year invite the campus safety officer from the environmental health and safety department (or its equivalent) to make a thorough facility inspection with you of all your playing areas. This report should identify things and areas needing repair, items to be removed, potential hazards, and suggestions for improvement. The report should be forwarded to your supervisor and key personnel in the operations and maintenance department. This should be followed up by a meeting of the appropriate departments to prioritize the items and establish who is responsible for the costs incurred.
3. Inform all physical education instructors, intercollegiate coaches,

participants, and others of the reporting lines to utilize in the process of having something repaired or to offer a suggestion.

4. Use supervisors (either professionals or students) to fill out facility report forms when making their rounds at games.
5. When visiting other recreation facilities, take a minute to observe how other universities run their programs, store equipment, clean their facilities, and so forth.
6. A safety committee made up of faculty and staff who are club advisors, instructors, and coaches can be very effective, because they are the specialists in their particular area and with their equipment. They also could be given the authority to make sure minor repairs are completed immediately and to follow up on incidents where an individual or group has been identified as being the cause for damaging property.
7. Other suggestions would include:
   - Have service agreements for weight lifting/gymnastic equipment.
   - Post emergency phones nearby.
   - Store all equipment (volleyball standards, basketball rebound boards, etc.) a safe distance from activities.
   - Make sure floors are clean, sprinkler heads are pushed down, and so forth.
   - Make sure facilities are properly lighted.
   - Make sure supervisors are properly trained (especially in CPR and first aid).

In summary, all sport club program administrators need to evaluate procedures frequently to make sure that, as reasonable and prudent professionals, they are making sure games are played on safe facilities.

TRAVEL PRACTICES AND LIABILITY CONCERNS IN SPORT CLUBS

Over the past several years, recreation specialists have become increasingly concerned with the aspects of the problem of liability injuries in intramural sports, sport clubs, and recreation programs.

Recreation departments nationwide have been trying fervently to insulate themselves against possible lawsuits concerning negligence. Unfortunately, few precedents, or prior cases that help to shape current court decisions, have pertained to intramural and recreational sports. This leaves the person in charge of administering campus recreation programs feeling somewhat frustrated. Our questions about liability issues are frequently met with answers such as: "There's been no precedent set on that issue, and until there is a lawsuit it's hard to say how a court will rule." Or,

"Have everyone participating in the activity sign a contractual release from liability, but it probably won't do any good in the event of a lawsuit." And worse yet, "To prevent any problems, abolish the activity," which we all tend to interpret as a sign that no activity is safe and we are not exempt from blame in a case of negligence. Yet the only way to eliminate the possibility of negligent lawsuits is to eliminate campus recreation entirely. There is no doubt that some lawyers (and possibly some administrators) would advocate this position.

Looking on the bright side, everyone is aware of the fact that with the fitness boom and recreation craze, campus recreation programs are expanding rapidly. Sport club programs, which in the past have been loosely organized, part of the student government, or totally unorganized, are increasingly becoming a part of the campus recreation department. With the drop of many varsity sports to club level and the growing involvement in new or different sports, liability in sport club programs is a concern for all campus recreation administrators.

Unlike intramural sports and open recreation or free-play activities, many sport clubs are competitive, extramural teams. The word "extramural" alone connotes the need to travel, thus conjuring up (in the minds of many administrators) ideas of speeding tickets, drunken parties at hotels, and demolished university vehicles. For this reason, campus recreation departments in charge of sport club operations have instituted several regulations regarding clubs' travel procedures. Many of these regulations are the university's rulings, but most rules are stipulations added by the controlling departments.

The majority of schools require, at minimum, five days advance notice when travel outside of the city is plannned. Fourteen days advance notice is not an uncommon stipulation. At Colorado State University, league schedules are kept on file so that a source of planned travel is available. However, this does not preclude clubs from making last-minute travel plans.

The type of advance notice ranges from verbal communication with the sport club or recreation director to authorization forms filled out by the club's president or in some cases each member of the traveling team. In addition, the university may require waivers signed by team members. In a few instances, travel forms must be sent to a dean or vice president for information or approval before the actual travel.

Because the majority of sport club operations are funded only in part by the university, most clubs that wish to travel must generate income for a portion of their trips. Often this means that clubs will elect to drive their own vehicles rather than rent cars or use motor pool vans. Regulations concerning use of personal vehicles range from simple notification of travel plans to an agreement signed before departure by the driver for use of a private vehicle. Several schools require owners of the vehicles to carry adequate liability and medical insurance coverage on the passengers and may also require coverage on drivers other than the owner. Adequate coverage is usually defined as the minimum insurance required by the state in which the vehicle is registered or a minimum specified by the school, such as $100,000 bodily injury coverage per person in the event of a lawsuit, $300,000 bodily injury per accident, and $100,000 property damage.

As an alternative to driving personal cars, many recognized student organizations are allowed to use vehicles from the university motor pool. Although securing transportation is generally considered to be the responsibility of the individual club, at some schools the sports club office will reserve vehicles for an off-campus trip.

One regulation that seems to apply to all schools is that a full-time faculty or staff member must accompany student organizations on trips outside of the city. At Colorado State, if more than one university vehicle is used, all vehicles must travel together in a caravan. Several universities require the driver to be an employee of the institution. In addition, a university motor pool may determine the qualifications of the driver. For example, if driving a specific size of van (i.e., one that seats more than 12 people) a certain driver's license is necessary. The screening of individual drivers may be done by the motor pool itself or by the recreation department. Other requirements may include reading a manual on use of university-owned vehicles, showing a current license of the type necessary, and signing an agreement for proper use and care of the vehicle. A few universities do not even carry collision insurance on their vehicles so the reponsibility of repairing damages is that of the driver.

Other rental of vehicles is less frequent but again, specific regulations apply. All leasing may be restricted to one agent, and a mix of university vehicles and private or leased vehicles on one trip may not be allowed. At Colorado State, whenever travel forms include intentions to rent vehicles, the university is required to provide insurance coverage in addition to that offered by the leasing agent. The clubs must pay for this coverage.

Other rules concerning travel vary from school to school and may include: a faculty advisor, sport club director, paid graduate assistant, or student supervisor to accompany a traveling club whenever possible; a limit on the number of vehicles taken per trip; written permission from the recreation department for nonclub members to travel with the team; and a report to the recreation department of any accidents or unusual happenings. Some colleges limit the distance a club may travel. Others allow men's and women's teams to travel together only when accompanied by an advisor.

When a university contracts with a licensed transportation company to transport students to and from a school-related activity, liability becomes the responsibility of the transportation agent. However, the use of student volunteers to drive vehicles or supervise programs will usually result in a liability situation in case of a participant injury. The courts will strain to find ultimate university responsibility even if a student uses his or her own car to drive a club to a university-sponsored event with no compensation. This is usually interpreted by the courts as a ''joint venture,'' part-time employment, or voluntary master-servant relationship.

Any student organization that is given even a small amount of university support and recognition should be considered a part of a university function. Campus recreation administrators should treat these clubs as integral to a university's function by taking responsibility for the organization and protection of student participants from potential harm.

Acknowledgment

This chapter was originally published in *Toward an understanding of intramural-recreational sports* (pp. 361-370) edited by B.C. Vendl, L.I. Hisaka, W.M. Holsberry, G.M. Maas, and M.J. Stevenson, 1984, Corvallis, OR: NIRSA. Copyright by NIRSA. Reprinted by permission.

BIBLIOGRAPHY

University of Denver. (1982-83). *Campus recreation sports clubs program*. Denver: Author.

Vanderbilt University. (1981-82). *Club sport handbook*. Nashville, TN: Author.

Colorado State University. (1982-83). *Club sports association student manual*. Fort Collins: Author.

Colorado State University. (1980-81). *Club sports handbook*. Ft. Collins: Author.

Purdue University. (1979-80). *Club sports handbook*. Lafayette, IN: Author.

University of Minnesota. (1978-79). *Recreational sports club officers' administrative workbook*.

East Carolina University. (1982). *Sport club information and guidelines manual*. Greenville, NC: Author.

Oregon State University. (1981). *Sports club policies and procedures*. Corvallis: Author.

University of California, Berkeley. (1980). *The university of California sports club program—constitution and by-laws*. Berkeley: Author.

PART V

Sport Club Program Surveys

Most administrators wish to know about administrative practices that existed in the past so they can gain direction for the present and the future. Knowledge of past practices may best be obtained through studying surveys. Trends in administrative techniques and the development of the sport club movement may also be determined from the data supplied by surveys.

This section consists of the results of four nationwide studies on sport club administration. The first, by the late Richard Jamerson of the University of North Carolina, was done in 1968. It was the definitive paper of its kind up to that time. A study carried out in 1969 resulted in the fulfillment of the PhD requirements by researcher Dale Phelps, then a graduate student at Indiana University. In 1980 while on sabbatical from the University of Illinois, Matthews chose to replicate the Phelps study, taking 2 years to do so, to determine trends in administrative processes as they pertain to sport club management. This sort of data analysis had never been attempted before. The time span of 13 years between the two studies was sufficiently long to determine clearly what trends and developments had taken place during that period.

The fourth and most recent survey was carried out by Buddy Goldhammer and Craig Edmonston in 1984. These two persons sent questionnaires to 46 institutions in the Big 8, Big 10, PAC 10, Southeast, and Southwest Athletic Conferences.

If one key trend has become evident through the data obtained by these surveys, it is that more and more educational institutions are appointing full-time persons to manage the sport club programs. Also, during the 13-year span between Phelps' doctoral study and my survey, the number of institutions centering the responsibility of sport club programming within the departments of campus recreation has increased dramatically. Additional support for this observation is seen in the fact that the 1986 *Recreational Sports Directory* published by the National Intramural-Recreational Sports Association lists about two thirds of all of its schools and colleges as having a person who is called the "Sports Club Director." The effect of the greater number of sport club directors is reflected in the increased time, money, and facilities allotted to sport clubs.

CHAPTER 15

Pros and Cons of Sport Clubs: A Survey—1968

Richard Jamerson
University of North Carolina

The history, philosophy, and organization of sport clubs has been written about fairly extensively. Likewise a variety of surveys, published and unpublished, have been made in an effort to find what the purpose is of such clubs, how are they organized, and what sports are involved, as well as a host of other details relating to this enduring interest in sports participation. In fact in 1968 this writer conducted a survey of 78 selected institutions, with the purpose of assisting in future policy decisions relative to sport club groups.

What has brought about the growth of sport clubs? Do students really want more opportunities to participate than now exist in intramural and recreation programs? Have we overorganized intramural programs and made our major form of recreation competitive whereas there are large interest groups who want to further their particular interests on a less organized basis? Or have intercollegiate sports become so highly organized and restrictive because of athletic scholarship participation that there is need to consider providing a more sane type of competitive program for the less highly skilled, unrecruited student athlete?

WHAT SPORTS ARE INVOLVED?

Some 75 different sports have club status, with the number in any single institution ranging from 0 to 40. The majority of the institutions have from three to eight clubs. Soccer and karate appear to enjoy the greatest popularity, with sailing, skiing, judo, fencing, gymnastics, and rugby not far behind. What one finds is a wide variety of sports interests among students, interests no doubt influenced by past experiences, geographical location of the institution, availability of facilities, availability of enough students with similar interest in forming a club, a fad of the times, or simply a desire to play and participate as a group with equally interested, skilled and socially acceptable individuals at a time suitable to those involved. This wide variety of interests and participation is not only encouraging but should be encouraged. Those of us responsible for sports programs gladly welcome more motor activity and less spectating. A word of caution would be that there is no reason to promote sport clubs at one institution because they exist at another; rather, let them develop naturally.

SPONSORSHIP OF SPORT CLUBS

Aside from self-sponsorship almost every type of agency on the college campus seems to be involved. The most common practice is for some member of the physical education intramural-athletic family to either initiate the club or take it under his or her wing after its initiation by students. Because the clubs are athletically oriented, need athletic facilities and equipment, and usually seek help from people in campus recreation, it is probably administratively easier for them to be sponsored, if sponsorship is necessary, by a campus recreation department rather than by some other campus agency.

With the present-day trend for students to always want to be involved in running the establishment, one wonders if this is not an area where students can be given a relatively free hand to organize and sponsor clubs that are relatively free from institutional direction and control. A partial answer relative to the feasibility or desirability of such practice may well depend upon the purpose of the club. For example, are these clubs a form of spontaneous student interest, are they being promoted for the purpose of trying to involve a greater number of students in sports activity, or are they a new approach to interschool sports?

One may well ask why they must be sponsored at all. Why is it not possible for students to have sport clubs in a free and unfettered atmosphere, their existence restricted only by the need for them to fit within the framework of the institution with respect to facilities?

It is not infrequently the philosophy of some intramural-recreation directors to sponsor more and more activities in an attempt to create the impression of great numbers of participants in the program. Is it quantity, often of the one-shot variety, we seek, or quality? Or is it a combination of both?

In general there appears to be confusion between what is meant by sponsorship and approval of sport clubs. The former apparently means the promotion of the club, and the latter approval of their right to exist under a set of rules.

APPROVAL OF THE CLUB TO FUNCTION

Club approval sometimes involves the previous issue, in that clubs may exist without approval but with sponsorship and vice versa. One finds many patterns, from no approval to a highly complicated plan involving an elaborate constitution and bylaws and an imposing list of governing regulations. If the institution requires approval of any type of campus organization, the sport clubs should adhere to such minimum requirements. Certainly a minimum of rules and regulations should suffice to permit the existence of this or any other voluntary interest group. We have enough highly complicated rules designed to control intercollegiate sports. It might be possible for the sport club area to provide some leadership toward a more sane and less complicated pattern of sports participation, particularly where interschool competition is involved. Surely there is no reason to have a cumbersome pattern involving rules and regulations and official interpretations of them to the extent that the unbridled interest of the student to play is reined in and destroyed. In essence—"let 'em play." Students interested in a sport may come to the gymnasium as a group and play day after day without any sponsorship or approval. In a sense they are a type of sport club that has long been in existence and will continue to be in existence without approval or sponsorship. As previously pointed out, the purpose of the club may provide the answer regarding the type of approval necessary for its existence.

FINANCING SPORT CLUBS

One finds a wide variety of practices, from no financing, to individual members paying dues, to partial or complete financing by some campus agency. The first question one may well ask is why any financing is necessary? If the institution approves the club and facilities and equipment are available, what other financing is necessary? Actually none, if a time and place to participate is all the club membership wants. On the other hand, the sport may be one for which there is no facility nor any equipment available; thus some budgeting problems exist. Also, as is frequently the case, the long-range interest of the group is to engage in competition with off-campus groups.

The general practice appears to be finding some financial means of helping sport clubs exist and attain their objectives. With reference to facilities and equipment, this is sound provided that proper consideration has been given to the need for such facilities and equipment in relation to long-range planning for expanding the total recreational opportunities for students and faculty. There would appear to be no justification in financing these clubs and not providing similar opportunities for students who have no interest in club membership but do have an interest in sports participation. A pitfall to avoid is trying to satisfy every interest group without taking time to evaluate their request for financial aid with respect to the possible continued interest in and need for the new club, as well as other administrative issues involved.

The question of competition with off-campus groups poses many problems, a sizable number involving more and more requests for financial assistance. If financing for this purpose is left entirely up to club members, then participation may depend in part upon the economic status of the student. Likewise, if a campus agency undertakes financial responsibility, much the same result occurs, and at some point some clubs will either receive no help, less help, or more help than others, depending upon the economic status of the financing agency.

It is true that intercollegiate programs have in some instances been expanded by sport clubs that become so strong that they are accepted as new intercollegiate teams. The intercollegiate sports budget already strained by football and basketball costs now has a greater strain. The sport club cost may not actually disappear, but there may now be a request to start another sport club in the same sport for the less talented but equally interested students, who eventually want a means of off-campus competition under a system of less severe rules and regulations.

One might elaborate indefinitely with specific illustrations of problems relating to financing sport clubs. It would appear that some clear definition is necessary of the purpose such clubs should and can serve if we are to make intelligent decisions relative to their existence and financial needs. Are they to be clubs whose major, if not only, purpose is to provide opportunity for those with like interests to participate free of organization and of the relatively restrictive rules in an institutional setting designed to provide recreational opportunities for its students, faculty, and employees? Or are they to be this plus a less formally organized intercollegiate athletic program? Are we moving toward two types of intercollegiate programs, the one we now have plus a new type involving teams who are self-coached and neither have nor want rules and will ultimately demand that which at the moment seems most important to their existence?

Financing sport clubs is one of the crucial issues in this new trend and cannot be easily resolved. In seeking an answer we might well learn from the experience of those in intercollegiate sports. Without some sound thinking relative to purpose, some definite direction, and some restraint upon individual desires to build a sport club empire, it is quite obvious that we will be faced with a host of perplexing problems in the very near future.

Despite the arguments of those who may say it represents a sign of the times, I have always felt that the expenditure of large sums of money to buy participation in sports is an unsound practice. If we provide facilities and equipment of sufficient quantity and organize and administer their use to the best advantage of the greatest number, is not this sufficient and less expensive financing?

FACILITIES, EQUIPMENT, AND INSTRUCTION FOR SPORT CLUBS

Because the same students are involved, only in a different setting, there would appear to be no reason to be concerned about facilities and equipment for this group beyond the already existing concern for all students. Certainly it would be a mistake for the institution to provide for these groups and not for others who wished to seek recreational opportunities as an individual and not as one of an organized group. Yet, one finds various patterns in existence, from no provision for facilities and equipment to complete provision.

Provision for instruction ranges from none to full-time, from members paying the cost of instruction to campus agencies paying part or all of the cost of sponsoring these clubs. Any answer to this issue must depend in part upon policy relating to all clubs on campus as well as the availability of funds for such programs. Unless there is some uniformity of policy and practice we will forever be tossing about on a sea of uncertainty.

Several interesting questions might be: (a) Why do students who oppose the required sports instruction program want and even seek instruction in sport clubs, and why are they willing to pay additional money for them? (b) Should consideration be given to reorganizing instructional programs on a sport club basis, or is this too idealistic? and (c) Would this be administratively possible within the framework of an educational curriculum?

SPECIFIC RULES FOR MEMBERSHIP IN SPORT CLUBS

One finds many suggestions and patterns for membership rules. Probably the most perplexing question relates to health clearance. Health standards governing eligibility for participation in intercollegiate sports are common practice in most institutions. Can or should such rules apply to sport clubs? Obviously they can, and possibly they should. On the other hand, no one is restricted from free, unorganized participation on the basis of his or her health status. Is there a point at which the individual should be permitted to make his or her own decisions relative to health status and recreational participation in athletic activities? Is there a dividing line between institutional and individual legal liability for what one does or what type of programs one participates in?

Beyond a possible solution of the health issue, any rules of an institutional nature, other than that the participant be a bona fide student, seem unjustified. If the institution permits or promotes any activity, then any student should be privileged to participate in such activity insofar as so-called general eligibility is concerned. There may, of course, be some specific rules indigenous to the group itself, but even they should be simple and not designed to clutter up the issue of who can and who cannot belong to the sport club.

Problems in this area seem to exist primarily where interschool competition is one purpose of the club. Even so, would it not be possible to use the "bona fide student" idea, thus eliminating the need for an elaborate set of rules for membership and participation such as presently exist in our intercollegiate programs?

PROBLEMS RELATIVE TO OFF-CAMPUS INTERSCHOOL COMPETITION

Problems about interschool competition are all related to purpose, finance, facilities, and similar questions. There are, however, a few specific issues that appear to present greater difficulty in the answering.

1. Who pays cost of travel? Presently, individual members, the club (from dues or appropriations), or some other agency pays the travel cost. Of concern is what is and should be involved—meals, travel, housing, contracts (guarantees), number of trips permitted, and so forth. A common practice is for the individual to pay such costs happily to get the program under-way, then soon expect the institution to take over this cost. At present there is no pattern of practice relating to this question.
2. Eligibility rules. The range is from none to many, which relate to academic eligibility, previous experience, and graduate, undergraduate, student, or faculty status. The bona fide student approach should cover this point, but rarely is this true. We seem to have a phobia for complicated rules of eligibility to participate in sports competition.

3. Who is legally responsible for what may happen during off-campus travel? Answers indicate (a) no one, (b) the individual, or (c) the institution. Are clubs officially representing the institution, or are they simply approved by the institution and function unofficially? To what extent is there legal responsibility? Does legal responsibility depend upon official approval, formal sponsorship, or mere existence of the club? This issue obviously needs thorough study before any answers will be forthcoming as a guide to policy and practice.
4. Do clubs travel as other athletic teams do or are they free from any regulations? They do everything at present, with a range from no regulations to the same as those for athletic teams.
5. Must clubs have a faculty representative? Yes and no—with many interpretations.
6. Are class absences granted for trips? Yes and no, depending upon whether or not the club is approved.
7. Must trips be approved? Yes and no, with many interpretations.
8. Do clubs officially represent the institution? Yes and no, depending upon local regulations relating to the points discussed in the previous paragraphs.

What one finds in this is no pattern of policy and practices but a lot of worrisome, perplexing problems about which we seem to be groping in the dark for answers. Basically we find ourselves attempting to answer these questions without any decision relative to the purpose of such organizations.

Most of the underlying issues would not exist in situations involving sport clubs unless interschool competition was one of the purposes of the club. Therefore, if we answer one question we answer many. On the other hand, if these clubs are to be a new type of off-campus competition group, then answers must be forthcoming. A sensible suggestion would be that we make no attempt to move in the direction of an NCAA of sport clubs, but rather that each institution answer these questions in line with institution policy and practice. Ask yourselves some questions. If the club pays travel costs on one campus and the institution pays on another campus, what difference does it make? If one institution has academic regulations, must another have the same? Is it always necessary to live as and keep up with the Joneses? The only issue that is really universal in importance is that of the legal, real, or moral responsibility of institutions for such groups traveling off campus.

One issue immediately raised by athletic coaches is that we can't have a set of training rules for our present varsity teams and another for sport club teams. In essence, if the sport club basketball team smokes, drinks beer, and has freedom, how can we control the varsity athlete? Space doesn't permit a real or philosophical discussion of this issue; however, changing times may provide some clues to an answer.

PRIORITY REGARDING USE OF FACILITIES

Everyone has a facilities problem. One of the major issues in many institutions regarding facility priority is the conflict of ideas about who and when one should use a facility. Physical education, intramural, and athletic personnel all too often think they "own" a facility. Fields standing unused and glistening green, restricted to athletics, intramurals, or men or women are an invitation to those looking for space for a new building or a parking lot. The first decision needed for determining priority of facilities is an administrator with the courage to make decisions and not be swayed by the ridiculous whim of individuals. Once this is done, priority relative to men, women, instruction, intramurals, intercollegiate sports, and recreation, as well as sport clubs, can be worked out. There must be adjustment of schedules, as well as sharing of use to the best advantage of all concerned. Someone is sure to be unhappy about a decision, but the fact remains that, insofar as possible, we have an obligation to provide, within reason, opportunity for all groups to share in the use of facilities and to use facilities for all groups.

The more one observes the growth and promotion of highly organized intramural programs the more one wonders if we may not be creating facility problems. If sport clubs are by chance a reaction to such highly organized programs, we may well need to consider this fact in deciding what course to pursue in the promotion of such clubs. If both types of programs are important but facilities are limited, we may need to limit each to keep things in balance.

THE PURPOSE OF SPORT CLUBS OVER AND ABOVE INTRAMURAL SPORTS

A variety of answers to the question of the purpose of sport clubs indicates in part some of the indecision relative to the purpose of such clubs as well as questions relating to problems created by their existence.

They serve the need for extramural experiences, are a halfway experience between intramural and intercollegiate athletics, involve sports not already in the program of intramurals, provide for special interest groups, serve as a way of starting a varsity sport, provide unorganized activity experiences, and meet the needs of the highly skilled who have an interest in a specific sport. This list might go on endlessly, but an analysis of many statements of purpose indicates that beyond the intramural program they

appear to fall into three main areas: (a) provision of additional sports opportunities on an unorganized basis, (b) a new form of interschool competition for students who are not satisfied with intramural experiences
yet do not wish to compete with recruited athletes or under a set of strict
rules, and (c) a gateway to varsity status. In a sense there is nothing new
in the sport club trend but rather just a broadening of what we already
have in one form or another. Thus, decisions relating to their purpose
and whether they should or should not exist are the same decisions we
have long been making as our programs expanded. Within the limits of
space, budget, and staff, we are all obviously interested in the development of such programs. On the other hand, does the institution have
a responsibility to try to satisfy every whim of students, or do we have
a need to reorient our thinking from the traditional intramural recreation
concept to a new and broader concept of sports participation?

It is quite easy for the student (or those promoting sport clubs) to argue
that this type of organization is needed. Before we jump on the bandwa-
gon we may well give some serious thought to all of the problems involved and to the questions of whether the needs are real or just a new
fad.

In one sense these clubs provide certain types of opportunities and experiences not normally a part of intramural-recreation programs, particularly where interschool competition is concerned. On the other hand,
they provide nothing new in that instruction is already available; recreational opportunities are unrestricted; intramural competition can, within limits, be expanded; and intercollegiate programs can have
junior-varsity teams that would provide greater opportunity for more
students to enjoy intercollegiate competition.

PROBLEMS CREATED BY THE PRESENCE
OF SPORT CLUBS

The question of problems created by sport clubs was included in my
survey, and appears to exist in other reports, to try to find out just what
seemed to be the stumbling blocks to such clubs. The major problems
appear to be: (a) how can such clubs be financed, (b) lack of space into
which they may be scheduled, (c) how to handle requests for interschool
competition, (d) the degree to which they are upsetting present programs,
and (e) who should be responsible for their approval and direction on
campus. Actually these are in a sense not new problems; they are simply
old problems in a new model. Their solution will rest upon evaluation
and determination of purpose of the club. In what frame of reference can
it exist on a given campus? Does it need financing, and if so, how can
it be financed within existing budgets? Is there space available for the

club to perform within the present program of activities? No one answer will suffice; in fact, there may be no universal answer at all. In all probability each problem will have to be resolved on an institutional basis. One thing is obvious; if we go off in every direction simply to satisfy what appear to be student interests, we may well create more problems than we solve.

Consideration may be given to the previously mentioned point that no new problems exist, but simply old ones in a new model. Therefore, rather than actually having problems to contend with we may instead have new purposes, ideas, and interests to consider. If this is true, do we remain unchanging or do we consider some new approaches to our whole concept of instruction, intramurals, recreation, and intercollegiate sports?

THE ORIGINAL TOPIC—
PROS AND CONS OF SPORT CLUBS

No one is basically opposed to the idea of sport clubs, with the main supporting reasons being more recreational opportunity, new sports participation opportunities not presently in existence on the campus, better opportunity to engage in sport of choice, serving minority groups, providing new competitive sports opportunities different from those presently available in intramural and intercollegiate programs, and providing intercollegiate sports program on a less highly organized basis. What is really being said is that we all encourage any type of sports participation that the students show a real interest in and that is administratively feasible.

But do we really believe or mean what we say when one considers the reasons opposing such clubs? They place a burden on the budget, there is no space for them, and we already have sports opportunities. Sport clubs can't be controlled, they fail unless someone keeps them organized and active, and they represent only fleeting interests of students and are not permanent unless "mothered" by some department. They are not income producing if engaged in interschool competition, and therefore they can't be afforded. Are we saying here, if we will be honest, that these clubs are fine but they are a nuisance, that we already have enough problems without creating more, and that we are already doing a good job so why clutter up the program with more of the same?

I suspect that a previous observation may apply here; namely, that we may need to reorient our thinking with respect to the whole area of intramurals, intercollegiate sports, and free recreational opportunities. We can rightly assume that intercollegiate sports in some form are going to continue to exist. Will that form be football, basketball, and all other sports; a certain number of sports highly promoted and others less highly promoted; or two distinct levels, one highly organized, the other footloose and fancy-free, as it were? Thus a real evaluation of the situation may provide some direction toward seeking answers to the questions that seem to be plaguing all of us relative to sport clubs.

An important issue facing us may well be just how far to go in organizing and promoting intramural competition. For example, it is easy to schedule all facilities for intramural games and leave none for free, unorganized programs. This might be one of the causes of the sudden interest in sport clubs. At the other end of the spectrum would be the sport clubs taking over the space at the expense of the intramural program. I can hear intramural directors screaming that this will never happen. Can you be sure the desire for unorganized competition will not be more challenging to students, if they are given the choice?

In one sense sport clubs are a fad and in another a serious desire of common sports interest groups to get together for play or competition. Under whatever guise or name, or for whatever purpose, sport clubs obviously represent an interest of people in sports participation. Therefore, we should intelligently cultivate this interest insofar as it represents expanded efforts to do what we are already trying to do within the limits of space, budget, and sound practice.

To oppose the idea is either to fail to recognize the interest of students toward a possible change of emphasis of present programs in intramural, intercollegiate, and recreational sports or reflective of a lack of ability to cope with the problems. We should neither shy away from the issues nor should we be rushed into seeking solutions. For the most part we will ultimately handle each situation with reference to our personal philosophy, the potentials existing in the institution we work for and ideas gleaned from meetings and discussion with our colleagues.

Acknowledgment

This chapter was originally published in *Proceedings of the 72nd annual meeting of the National College Physical Association for Men* (pp. 41-49) by R.E. Jamerson, 1969. Reprinted by permission.

CHAPTER 16

A Comparison of the Results of the Matthews Survey of 1982 and Data From the Phelps Survey of 1969

David O. Matthews
University of Illinois

The following are the results of a 1982 survey of United States and Canadian institutions listed in the 1982 *NIRSA Directory* as having a sport club program on their campuses. A detailed questionnaire (see appendix C) was sent to campus recreation directors at 299 colleges and universities. The return rate was 66%, with 199 institutions responding.

The questionnaire was a replication of the one used by Dr. Dale Phelps in his doctoral study, which he completed in 1970 at the University of Indiana.* The decision to replicate the study was based on the opinion that trends in certain aspects of sport club administration could be determined as they occurred over a 13-year span. Phelps collected his data in 1969 from 60 schools in Illinois, Indiana, Michigan, Ohio, and Wisconsin.

The data will be presented first in this report. Comparisons of similarities and differences of the data will then be made where there seems to be some significance in the comparisons. (The symbol ** indicates a significant item.)

---

*Dr. Phelps is Director of Physical Education at Northern Michigan University.

THE ADMINISTRATION OF SPORT CLUBS

Statement or question	Matthews	Phelps
I. Philosophy		
1. The sport club program should be student directed.	64% agree or strongly agree	60% agree or strongly agree
2. Sport clubs, particularly the team sports, are a good source of new intercollegiate sports.	58% agree or strongly agree	75% agree or strongly agree
3. Many of the existing sport clubs generate the majority of their matches and competition on an intraclub basis.	56% agree or strongly agree	65% agree or strongly agree
4. Each registered sport club should be given a specific financial appropriation to run its own program.	72% agree or strongly agree	65% agree or strongly agree
5. A sport club competing on an intercollegiate basis is generally administratively feasible.	68% agree or strongly agree	60% agree or strongly agree
6. The sport club program is a part of the total intramural program.	52% agree or strongly agree	57% agree or strongly agree
7. The intramural department should *not* be involved with the sport club program.	58% disagree or strongly disagree	60% disagree or strongly disagree
8. Whenever possible, sport clubs are assisted in making the transition to intercollegiate athletics.**	53% agree or strongly agree	76% agree or strongly agree
9. Comments.		
II. Registration and Institutional Sanction		
10a. Are sport clubs officially recognized by the President, Board of Regents, and so forth in the institution?	78% yes	73% yes
10b. Are sport clubs officially recognized by other administrators within the institution?	91% yes	91% yes
11a. Is there a person in the institution designated as the coordinator or a liaison for the club program?**	83% yes	55% yes
11b. Indicate your title and/or department.		
1) Intramural Director	34%	51%
2) Assistant Intramural Director	21%	—
3) Sport Club Coordinator	15%	3%
4) Director of Athletics	7%	15%
5) Director of Student Activities	3%	18%

12. Which department(s) within the institution is(are) responsible for the administration of the sport club program?

a) Intercollegiate Athletics	20%	17%
b) Intramurals	43%	31%
c) Military (ROTC)	2%	2%
d) Office of Student Affairs	37%	20%
e) Physical Education	18%	15%
f) Recreation Department	27%	23%
g) Student Union	14%	11%
h) Student Senate	13%	1%
i) Student Finance Committee	11%	2%

13. Is each sport club required to file

a) a written constitution?	83% yes	69% yes
b) a list of elected officers?**	88% yes	68% yes
c) a list of all club members?**	74% yes	53% yes

14a. Does each sport club have an advisor?   87% yes   95% yes

14b. Is the advisor selected by the club members?   79% yes   77% yes

14c. If the advisor is appointed, by whom?

1) Director of Athletics	36%	26%
2) Director of Intramurals	28%	21%
3) Administering Department	17%	15%
4) Department Chair	6%	5%
5) Interested faculty professor	31%	5%

14d. Is the advisor a faculty member?   90% yes   94% yes

14e. Is the advisor usually a member of the faculty of the administering department?   80% yes   68% yes

15. May a registered sport club in good standing officially use the name of the institution as a part of the recognized name of the club?   95% yes   93% yes

16. May official recognition of a sport club be withdrawn for violation of institutional regulations?   87% yes   95% yes

17a. Does your institution have a sport club council?   68% no   95% no

17b. Indicate the council's functions.

1) Establish policies	86%	No data
2) Revise general regulations pertaining to sport clubs	83%	No data
3) Serve as a liaison between sport clubs and coordinator of the program	80%	No data
4) Determine budget	63%	No data
5) Evaluate program	70%	No data
6) Schedule activities	70%	No data

Statement or question	Matthews	Phelps
18. Comments.		
19. Of the 43 clubs listed in the questionnaire indicate		
a) which clubs were active.	All clubs except soaring were active in 1981-82.	Horse polo, water skiing, and wrestling were *not* active in 1967-68.
b) which clubs competed on an interclub basis.	All clubs except soaring competed in 1981-82.	Basketball, touch football, horseback riding, horse polo, water skiing, softball, square dance, and wrestling did *not* compete in 1967-68.
c) which clubs were corecreational.	All clubs but soaring were corecreational in 1981-82.	Lacrosse, horse polo, rowing, rugby, water skiing, soccer, softball, squash, track, water polo, weight lifting, wrestling, cricket, touch football, handball, and ice hockey were *not* corecreational in 1967-68.
19d. The average membership was	25 members in 1981-82	21 members in 1967-68

III. Eligibility

Statement or question	Matthews	Phelps
20. Are the following individuals eligible for sport club membership?		
a) Undergraduate students	100% yes	100% yes
b) Graduate students	81% yes	63% yes
c) Faculty members	72% yes	55% yes
d) Alumni**	70% no	90% no
e) Nonacademic staff**	63% yes	69% no
21a. Are there specific scholastic requirements for club membership?	74% no	72% no
21b. If any, are the scholastic requirements for clubs as stringent as those of the NCAA?	66% no	61% no
22a. Are sport club members eligible for intramural competition in the sport represented by their club?	71% yes	74% yes
22b. Is there a limit as to the number of club members on the same team?	52% yes	64% yes
23. Are members of aquatic activity clubs required to pass a basic swimming test?	55% no	70% yes

IV. Finance

24a. Do sport club members pay dues?	81% yes	56% yes
24b. If dues are paid, what are the minimum and the maximum assessments?	Minimum $2, median $8.20, maximum $40+	Minimum $2, median $3.39, maximum $20
25. Is the sport club program partially financed by		
a) general student fee?	64% yes	49% yes
b) budget of administering department?	48% yes	62% yes
c) gate receipts of club contests?	70% no	78% no
d) fund-raising projects?**	85% yes	39% yes
e) commercial grants?	85% no	No data
f) gifts?	61% yes	No data
26. Do sport clubs have advisors?	92% yes	No data
a) Are club advisors paid for their services?	90% no	93% no
1) How much per hour, if paid?	$6.20	$6.40
b) Are club advisors given a decreased load in teaching, administration, or coaching?	97% no	91% no
27a. Are non-university personnel utilized to give lessons to club members?	79% no	58% yes
27b. Are these non-university persons paid by the club for their services?**	51% no	74% no
28a. Is the sport club treasurer required to keep a record of all business transactions?	84% yes	83% yes
28b. Are these financial records subject to audit by institutional officials?	86% yes	69% yes
28c. Is the treasurer required to receive the advisor's approval or signature before writing a pay voucher or check?	71% yes	58% yes
29. Does the institution accept the financial responsibility for individual club debts?	65% no	No data
30. What was the fiscal year operatting budget?	$6,000	$1,500

V. Medical Supervision

31a. Are all members of the contact sport clubs required to have physical exam results on file with the student health service?	71% no	53% no
31b. Are members required to sign an accident liability release form?**	53% yes	20% yes

Statement or question	Matthews	Phelps
31c. Are parents or guardians of club members under 21 years of age required to sign a liability release form?	75% no	82% no
31d. Is an injury report form available to record all injuries resulting from participation in sport club activities?	74% yes	71% yes
31e. Is medical treatment provided at the student health center for injuries resulting from sport club practice sessions and contests?	87% yes	95% yes
31f. Is a *student* athletic trainer present at all interclub home contests involving contact sports?	81% no	66% no
31g. Is a student trainer present at practices of contact sports?	86% no	88% no
31h. Is an athletic trainer present at all interclub *home* contests involving contact sports?	83% no	75% no
31i. Is a physician present at all interclub *home* contests involving contact sports?	96% no	95% no
31j. Is a physician present at all practice sessions involving contact sports?	99% no	98% no
31k. Is the institution financially responsible for injuries resulting from sport club practices and games?	83% no	84% no
31l. Does the institution subscribe to liability insurance to protect employees and club advisors against suits invoked for injuries incurred during practices and games?	69% yes	60% yes
31m. Is a medical examination required before a player is permitted to return to the sport following illness or injury?	76% no	67% no
32a. Is student health insurance available?	91% yes	No data
32b. Is the insurance mandatory?	67% no	No data

VI. Equipment and Facilities

33. Do club members provide all of their own personal equipment?	62% yes	63% yes
34. Does your institution furnish any of the following equipment to clubs?		
a) Ammunition	88% no	87% no
b) Archery	89% no	87% no
c) Balls	62% yes	60% yes

d) Bats	77% no	80% no
e) Paddles and racquets	81% no	73% no
f) Shoes, cleated	99% no	85% no
g) Shoes, tennis	99% no	98% no
h) Skis	92% no	98% no
i) Shuttlecocks	81% no	82% no
j) Uniforms, practice	87% no	62% no
k) Uniforms, game	60% no	48% no
35. Does your institution provide a capital outlay for initial and basic equipment for clubs?	51% no	55% no
36a. Are facilities owned and operated by the institution available for club use?	99% yes	98% yes
36b. Are these facilities all provided free of charge?	70% yes	57% yes
36c. Do bowling lanes, golf courses, ice rinks, and ski slopes generally charge for use?	100% yes	100% yes
37a. Are lockers available for members?	79% yes	82% yes
37b. If lockers are available are they free of charge?	72% yes	57% yes
37c. Is towel service free of charge?**	68% no	47% no

VII. Interclub Competition

38. Do sport clubs engage in interclub competition?	97% yes	95% yes
39. Which of the following are sources of competition for your club teams?		
a) Other sport club teams	97%	95%
b) Intercollegiate teams	70%	87%
c) YMCA teams	19%	20%
d) AAU teams	33%	18%
e) Sport days	19%	1%
40. Does your institution permit sport clubs to establish conference or league affiliations?	80% yes	51% yes
41a. Does an administrator give final approval for all sport club competitive schedules?	61% yes	56% yes
41b. Who gives the final approval for all sport club competitive schedules?		
1) Director of Athletics	20% no	25% yes
2) Director of Intramurals	32% yes	25% yes
3) Chair of Department of Physical Education	10% yes	10% yes
4) Student Activities Office	17% yes	1% yes
5) Club Advisor**	43% yes	8% yes
41c. Are these schedules limited as to the number of games per season a team can play?	55% no	57% no

Statement or question	Matthews	Phelps
42. Does the administering department assume the total expense incurred for interclub competition including		
a) game equipment?	73% no	58% no
b) game officials?	60% no	50% no
c) lodging for visiting team members?	95% no	92% no
d) meals for visiting team members?	97% no	90% no
e) portable bleachers, erection and removal?	73% no	69% no
f) public address system?	70% no	65% no
g) use of facility?	64% yes	74% yes
43. Are sport clubs permitted to charge admission to their home contests?**	64% yes	40% yes
44. Do sport clubs derive income from concessions sold at interclub contests?	64% no	81% no
45. Are local news media permitted to use such terms as "varsity," "returning lettermen," and so forth when referring to sport club team members?	79% no	61% no

VIII. Travel

Statement or question	Matthews	Phelps
46. Do teams travel for interclub competition?	100% yes	95% yes
47a. Is team travel for interclub competition restricted during the regular season?	60% no	45% no
47b. Maximum distance allowed for competition	over 1,000 miles	over 1,000 miles
48a. Does an administrator give the approval to sport club travel?	73% yes	58% yes
48b. Who gives the final approval?		
1) Director of Athletics	18% yes	28% yes
2) Director of Intramurals	26% yes	25% yes
3) Chair of Department of Physical Education	7% yes	1% yes
4) Sport Club Coordinator**	37% yes	3% yes
5) Student Activities Office	17% yes	10% yes
6) Dean of Students	8% yes	3% yes
7) Faculty Advisor	21% yes	5% yes
49a. Who provides the vehicle for off-campus travel to competition?		
1) Public carrier	31% yes	22% yes
2) Student cars	79% yes	70% yes
3) Institution	64% yes	47% yes
49b. If a student provides a car is he or she required to have mini-	57% no	50% no

mum bodily injury liability and property damage liability automobile insurance coverage?

50a. Are sport club members given an expense allowance for lodging on overnight trips?	70% no	72% no
50b. Are sport club members given an expense allowance for meals enroute to and from contests?	73% no	60% no
50c. Is the advisor required to make all trips with the club?	68% no	46% no
50d. May another approved adult substitute for the advisor on trips?	74% yes	54% yes
50e. Are coed club members permitted to travel with the club team?**	88% yes	53% yes
50f. Is interclub competition scheduled only on weekends?	77% no	57% no
50g. Do members of traveling club teams receive excused absences for classes missed during trips away from the campus for interclub competition?	74% no	61% no

COMPARISON OF RESULTS

My intent is to attempt to draw *some* conclusions about the differences between the data presented by Phelps and that which I have accumulated. One may assume that such things as new rules and regulations, legal liability, and shifting mores have effected changes in the administration of sport clubs on the campuses of the universities and colleges. I will make certain assumptions based on my knowledge of sport club programming and on the writings of experts in the field.

A difference of 20 percentage points between the data from the two surveys was arbitrarily selected as indicating that there is some degree of significance between the two sets of data. It is to be noted that where "no data" is indicated in these results it is because of insufficient returns for those particular questions.

Under Section I, "Philosophy," the statement was "Whenever possible, sport clubs are assisted in making the transition to intercollegiate sports." Of Phelps' respondents, 76% strongly agree or agree to the statement while 53% of the 1982 respondents strongly agree or agree. From the comments made by the persons who answered the 1982 questionnaire, it appears that directors feel the number of sport clubs is so great and diversified and the aim of sport clubs is so different from that of intercollegiate sport programs that they have little desire to promote varsity status for the clubs. On the other side, the athletic directors are faced with the many problems of financing the existing intercollegiate sport programs for both men and women, and so they generally do not feel that they can afford to take on the financial responsibility of additional varsity sports. In Section II, "Registration and Institutional Sanction," question 11a asked, "Is there a person in the institution designated as the coordinator or a liaison for the club program?" The difference between the data is a reflection of the tremendous growth of the sport club program during the 13 years between surveys. University and college administrators have dealt with burgeoning numbers of sport organizations on campuses and numerous program problems. It has become imperative that some unit on campus, and specifically some person, be named to head up the administration of the sport clubs.

Question 13 of this same section asked, "Is each sport required to file (a) a written constitution, (b) a list of elected officers, and (c) a list of all club members?" During the late 1960s, the general requirement that clubs submit lists of officers and club members was rescinded in many institutions upon the insistence of student groups. Since that time, there has been a gradual return to the requirement. This would possibly explain the differences in the two sets of data.

In Section III, "Eligibility," it was indicated in question 20d that in 1982 20% fewer schools have clubs that allow alumni to be members of sport clubs. One explanation for this difference could be that there are more clubs with more members and facilities are being taxed to their utmost. More graduate students, faculty members, and very notably (Section III, question 20e) nonacademic personnel have increased the number of members of clubs. This increase puts a tremendous burden on existing facilities. In spite of the fact that the intervening 13 years saw a remarkable increase in the number of new facilities constructed throughout the United States and Canada, there remains a great need for additional ones. Until the facilities meet the needs of the clubs, restrictions of some type will have to be put into effect on a priority basis.

In Section IV, "Finance," question 25d shows that since 1969 more clubs are using fund-raising projects to assist them in financing their activities. Even though the 1982 survey shows more clubs are receiving student fee money (question 25a), fewer administering departments are providing funds for the clubs. These two facts, combined with the increase in the number of clubs on the campuses, indicate that there are fewer dollars per club to be allocated. It is also true that the clubs that compete, which need funds for uniforms, travel, and other expenses, demand and receive the greater bulk of the available money.

A further reflection on the tightness of dollars per capita (membership) is shown in Section III, question 27b, which indicates that since 1969 there has been a decrease in the number of clubs that hire nonmembers to give lessons in that club's activities. Apparently, club officers and members feel that there is enough expertise within the clubs for purposes of instruction.

Many more institutions of higher education are aware of the legal liability suits that have been brought against any and all administrative personnel within a college or university. As more and more students become involved in club activities, especially those of a high-risk nature, administrators are searching for ways to reduce or eliminate liability for injury or death that occurs to any club member or affiliate. The question about accident liability release forms (Section IV, "Medical Supervision," question 31b) shows that 33% more institutions are requiring club members to fill out this type of form. The accident liability release form does not release an institution from all fault, but it often discourages claims, and some courts have rules that they are legally valid.

The cost of laundering towels has increased since 1969. This, combined with the fact that departments have less money to give to clubs, may be the reason why, according to question 37c, more schools are charging the clubs for towel service.

Question 40 in Section VII, "Interclub Competition," "Does your institution permit sport clubs to establish conference or league affiliations?" elicited the data that 29% more clubs belong to competitive leagues or associations in 1982 than in 1969. The attractiveness of belonging to a conference or league is that one finds in the intercollegiate program ease of scheduling, traditional rivalries, similar aims, and more equal competition. These are just some of the reasons why membership in a league is desired more and more by competitive clubs.

If a club advisor is doing the job properly, that person is probably more aware of the demands of a competitive schedule than other administrators on campus. The great increase in the responsibility of approving schedules, increasing from 8% in 1969 to 43% in 1982, being given to the club advisor may be a recognition by campus administrators of this fact.

Question 43 of Section VII shows that a greater percentage of clubs are being allowed to charge admission for their home contests. This could be because of the financial changes that have occurred in the financing of club programs.

With 28% more institutions naming a coordinator of sport clubs to oversee the programs of these student organizations, it is only logical that the data in Section VIII, "Travel," question 48b, item 4 would show that the sport club coordinator is the person who, more than any other, gives final approval allowing the sport club to travel to a site for interclub competition. Because in 1982 17% more schools are allowing clubs to use their vehicles, it is only common sense that these institutions would want to control their usage as much as possible.

Questions 50e and 50f provided evidence to the fact that since 1969 more and more institutions of higher education are removing themselves from the status of in loco parentis and therefore not putting themselves in the position of judging ethical issues. At one time, almost all sport clubs were "men-only" organizations. Now, with the advent of coeducational sport club programs, the women are given the same rights and considerations, as well as privileges, that formerly were accorded only to male students. Women club members are permitted to travel with the club team in 88% of the schools. In conjunction with the idea that schools are not as closely involved with moral and religious matters, more colleges and universities are lifting the ban on weekend travel, which in many instances would include competing on Sundays.

REFERENCES

Phelps, D.E. (1970). *Current practices and recommended guidelines for the administration of sports clubs in selected four-year midwest colleges and universities*. Unpublished doctoral dissertation, Indiana University, Bloomington.

CHAPTER 17

Comparison of University Sport Club Programs in the Big 8, Big 10, PAC 10, Southeastern, and Southwest Athletic Conferences, 1984

Buddy Goldammer
Craig Edmonston
University of Arkansas, Fayetteville

How many times during the school year are intramural directors asked questions concerning their sport club programs by their superiors, students, and other intramural professionals? Questions concerning budgets, liability, transportation, number and kinds of clubs, administrative organization, and participation numbers are commonplace.

The past several years have seen major changes in sport club administration, partly because of necessary budget decreases. Today, it is vitally important for the sport club director to be knowledgeable about the current status of sport club programs throughout the United States. With this knowledge, the sport club director can support budget and program increases, defend budget and program decreases, compare program offerings, and make budget and administrative comparisons. The data from surveys such as this can serve a variety of purposes for the sport club director.

PURPOSE

The purpose of this study was to determine the current status of sport club programs in the intramural recreational sports programs of the Big 8, Big 10, PAC 10, Southeast, and Southwest Athletic Conferences. More specifically, this study was designed to give the sport club director data concerning (a) types of clubs, (b) number of clubs and programs, (c) types of administration, (d) methods of finance, (e) eligibility requirements, (f) travel regulations, (g) liability and insurance coverage, (h) advertisement and promotion methods, and (i) methods of faculty/staff sponsorship.

METHODOLOGY

The 41-question survey was mailed to each university in the Big 8, Big 10, PAC 10, Southeast, and Southwest Athletic Conferences. A follow-up survey was mailed to each university not responding within 30 days. A total of 46 universities were selected to participate in the study. Responses were received from 44 universities, for a 95% response. One university from the Big 10 and the Southeast Conference failed to respond.

Responses to each question were tabulated by university and then compiled to show composite results according to conference. Tabulated conference responses were compiled to indicate total responses to each question. When respondents indicated the "other" response to a question, the response was listed in both the conference and composite conference results.

RESULTS

All respondents to the survey indicated that they sponsor a sport club program. The composite results indicated that 7% of the respondents sponsored 41 or more clubs, 23% sponsored 31 to 40 clubs, 14% sponsored 21 to 30 clubs, 34% sponsored 11 to 20 clubs, and 23% sponsored 10 clubs or fewer. The average number of clubs sponsored by the respondents was 16 to 25.

The number of clubs sponsored varied considerably according to conference. The Big 10 Conference sponsored the largest number of clubs, with the average number of clubs per university being 29 to 38, followed by the PAC 10 with 17 to 26 clubs per university. The Southeast Conference averaged 12 to 21 clubs per university, the Big 8 Conference averaged 10 to 21 clubs per university, and the Southwest Conference averaged 10 to 20 clubs per university (see Table 1).

The composite results indicated that 106 different sport clubs were sponsored by the respondents. The ten most common sports for which a club was sponsored, are listed in Table 2.

Rugby, fencing, volleyball, judo, and Frisbee were the only sports for which clubs were sponsored by all respondents in the Big 10 Conference. Rugby and soccer were the club sports sponsored by all respondents in

Table 1
Number of Sport Clubs Sponsored
by Universities in Each Conference

Number of Clubs	Big 10	PAC 10	Southeast	Big 8	Southwest
0-10	—	—	2	4	4
11-20	1	6	4	1	3
21-30	2	2	1	1	—
31-40	3	2	1	2	2
40-55	3	—	—	—	—

Table 2
Ten Most Sponsored Clubs
(44 Universities Responded to Survey)

Clubs	Number of Universities Sponsoring
Rugby	42
Soccer	40
Fencing	33
Karate	33
Sailing	31
Volleyball	31
Lacrosse	29
Judo	27
Water Polo	27
Frisbee	26

the PAC 10 Conference. In the Southeast Conference, rugby, karate, soccer, and water skiing were the only clubs sponsored by all respondents. The Big 8 respondents indicated rubgy as the only sport sponsored by each university, and the Southwest Conference did not have a club sport that was sponsored by all respondents.

Membership numbers in the various sport club programs varied considerably according to conference. The Big 10 Conference had the largest membership with range of 1,201 to 2,278 participants per university. The PAC 10 Conference had a range of 711 to 1,400 participants per university. Universities in the Southeast Conference had a range of participation from 288 to 713. The Big 8 Conference universities ranged from 376 to 900 participants, and the Southwest Conference ranged from 256 to 700. The composite results indicated that 5% of the respondents had a membership of 2,001 or more, 32% had a membership of 1,000 to 2,000, 19% had a membership of 501 to 1,000, 12% had a membership of 301 to 500, and 32% had a membership of 300 or fewer. The average membership of all respondents was 535 to 1,152 participants.

Of the 44 respondents, 40 indicated that a written constitution/bylaws is required of each sport club. One university in each of the Big 10, PAC 10, Big 8, and Southwest Conferences did not require a written constitution.

Of the 44 respondents, 40 permitted faculty/staff members to belong to their clubs, 15 permitted alumni to belong, 12 permitted community residents to belong, and 44 permitted clubs to determine membership policies. All respondents permitted student memberships.

The composite results showed that 22 of the 44 respondents allowed only registered university students to participate. Of the 22 respondents that specified registered students, only 13 required a specific number of registered hours. Of the 44 respondents, 16 permitted clubs to determine eligibility requirements, 26 permitted sport club members to participate in the same sport in intramurals, and 18 did not permit participation in the same intramural sport.

Twenty-six of the 44 respondents indicated that they had a director of sport clubs. Of those 26, 20 required that the director be a full-time professional, 4 permitted part-time professionals, 2 had student directors, and 2 had assigned physical education/recreation faculty as directors. The Big 10 was the only conference that restricted the sport club director to being a full-time professional.

The composite results indicated that the sport club directors reported to a variety of administrative personnel, depending on the administrative organization of the program. Twenty-seven of the 44 respondents reported directly to the director of recreational sports. The remaining respondents reported to the administrative chair of the controlling college or student affairs program.

A sport club council or advisory board was utilized by 27 of the 44 respondents. Of the 27 respondents using councils or boards, 11 were comprised of students and faculty/staff, 14 were comprised of students only, and two were comprised of the club presidents. The members of the councils or boards were elected in 13 of the 27 responding universities utilizing councils or boards. The remainder were appointed by the director of recreational sports, the director of sport clubs, or the president or vice president of the institution.

A club advisor was required by 34 of the 44 respondents. Nine respondents recommended but did not require club advisors, and one respondent had no requirements for club advisors. All universities in the Southeast and Southwest Conferences required club advisors, but universities in the other conferences either required or recommended, or did not require or recommend club advisors. Of the 34 respondents requiring club advisors, 28 specified that the club advisor must be a qualified faculty/staff member. The remaining 6 respondents allowed anyone who was interested in assuming the responsibility to be club advisor.

Funding for the sport club programs was primarily through student activity fees; 23 of the 44 respondents funded sport clubs in this manner. Eight respondents funded through general university funds, and nine respondents used a combination of student activity fees and general university funds. The remaining four respondents funded through student government funds, dues, or fund-raising projects. The composite results indicated that when clubs raised funds, 41 of the 44 respondents did so through fund-raising projects, 38 collected dues, 36 solicited contributions, and 15 utilized alumni programs.

The composite results indicated that the average sport club program budget was $24,159 to $32,226. The composite results also indicated that 7% did not fund clubs, 2% funded $3,000 to $4,000, 27% funded $5,000 to $9,999, 20% funded $10,000 to $19,999, 25% funded $20,000 to $30,000, 2% funded $30,000 to $40,000, 2% funded $40,000 to $50,000, 11% funded $50,000 to $60,000, and 1% funded $60,000 to $70,000, $80,000 to $90,000, $90,000 to $100,000, and $130,000 to $134,000 respectively.

The average Big 10 Conference budget was $35,555 to $42,221. The PAC 10 Conference's average budget was $24,500 to $32,999. The average Southeast Conference budget was $22,875 to $29,240. The average Southwest Conference budget was $21,111 to $28,777, and the average Big 8 Conference budget was $13,750 to $19,999.

Of the 44 respondents, 31 did not have restrictions on travel or allowed travel distances. The remaining 13 respondents had regulations specifying geographical regions, budget restrictions, and type of tournament. Thirty-three of the 44 respondents did not have regulations governing competition opponents. Eleven allowed competition against sport clubs only. Twenty of the 44 respondents permitted a club officer to supervise a trip, 17 required the advisor to accompany and supervise a trip, and 7 did not have trip supervision regulations.

The composite results indicated that 22 of the 44 respondents required a signed liability release form before participation with a club. Seven respondents utilized an informal form, and 11 did not require a liability release form. Thirty of the 44 respondents indicated that liability insurance was not provided for sport club participants. Eleven of the respondents indicated that liability insurance was provided by the institution for sport club participants. Twenty-five of the 44 respondents indicated that liability coverage for advisors was not provided. Eighteen respondents indicated that advisor liability coverage was provided by the institution.

Participant medical coverage was provided by 5 of the 44 respondents. Twenty-nine respondents indicated that the participants had to furnish their own medical coverage, and 13 respondents did not require medical coverage for club participants.

Twenty-three of the 44 respondents indicated that they did not have paid advertising for their sport club program, and 21 indicated that they did. Seventeen of the 21 respondents using paid advertising had a sport club brochure and the student newspaper as their primary promotional tools. Eleven respondents also utilized an intramural newsletter as a form of advertisement.

As an accident recording method, 30 of the 44 respondents indicated that accident forms must be completed for all accidents. Eleven respondents did not use accident forms, and three used accident forms only occasionally. Eleven respondents indicated that club participants were required to sign forms indicating knowledge of safety regulations. Thirty respondents did not require safety regulation forms, and three used them only on occasion.

The composite results indicated that 37 of the 44 respondents evaluated their programs on a periodic basis. Four respondents indicated that they did not evaluate their programs on a periodic basis, and three respondents indicated that they evaluated their programs only occasionally.

DISCUSSION

Several statements can be made about the results. It is clear that the sport club program is a vital part of the total intramural field, both to the professional and to the individual participant. Considerable amounts of time and money are utilized to administer a sport club program. Thousands of students, faculty, and staff participate in sport clubs in the Big 10, PAC 10, Big 8, Southeast, and Southwest Conferences alone.

The size of the program greatly influences the budget, administrative organization, number of staff, and general policies. Students are given the opportunity to participate, not only in their chosen area of interest, but in the administration of the program. Activities are made available that are impossible or impractical to include in other areas of university life. The sport club program also allows the faculty/staff member to participate and associate with students outside the educational arena.

Acknowledgment

This chapter was originally published in *Interpretive aspects of intramural-recreational sports* (pp. 225-230) edited by B.C. Vendl, D.C. Dutler, W.M. Holsberry, T.C. Jones, and M. Ross, 1984, Corvallis, OR: NIRSA. Copyright by NIRSA. Reprinted by permission.

Appendices

Sport Club Information and Guidelines Manual

Robert A. Fox

The following pages were selected from the sport club manual assembled by Robert A. Fox when he was director of campus recreation at East Carolina University. Bob Fox had collected sport club handbooks from several hundred colleges and universities and used them, along with what he had already composed, to put together a comprehensive handbook for the sport clubs on his campus.

The following excerpts from the East Carolina University Guidelines Manual are representative of what any sport club supervisor could put into his or her manual or handbook. The table of contents for the entire manual is included here to give to the reader a more comprehensive understanding of the scope of a manual of this type.

SPORT CLUB MANUAL

Table of Contents

Executive Council
Meeting Dates

V. **Bylaws**

VI. **Budget**
Allocated Funds
Nonallocated Funds

VII. **Membership and Eligibility**

VIII. **Membership Dues**

IX. **Officer Responsibilities**
President
Vice President/Secretary
Treasurer
Members

X. **Advisor**

XI. **Coach**

XII. **Meetings**

XIII. **Sports Medicine Policies**

XIV. **Trainer Coverage**

XV. **Scheduling of Competition, Special Events, Tournaments, and Exhibitions**

XVI. **Facilities**
Request
Usage
Special Events
Keys

XVII. **Equipment**
Purchase
Storage
Inventory
Utilization
Administration

XVIII. **Training Supplies**

XIX. **Office Equipment and Supplies**

XX. **Travel**

XXI. **Publicity**

XXII. **Fund-Raising**

XXIII. **Secretarial Assistance**

XXIV. Telephone Usage

XXV. Evaluation

XXVI. Club Conduct

XXVII. Yearbook

SPORTS MEDICINE POLICIES

East Carolina University Sport Club participation is completely voluntary. As such, each member assumes responsibility for injuries and subsequent results of injuries, that may occur. The University shall not be responsible for treatment of defects or injuries that occur during this participation or that become apparent after the individual is no longer a club member.

To reduce the chance for misunderstandings concerning University responsibility, each member of the various Sport Clubs using University facilities should become familiar with these statements concerning University and club member responsibility.

1. Each member of a sport club must sign a Liability Release/Waiver and Assumption of Risk Certificate before being able to participate in *any* club activity. This form states that each Sport Club Member realizes there is a risk of injury while participating and that the Department of Intramural-Recreational Services is not responsible for any injury that occurs during this sport. Sport club members who are under 18 years of age must have a parent or guardian sign the Release/Waiver and Assumption of Risk Certificate before being able to participate in *any* club activity.

2. Each club member of a sport club must have proof of adequate medical insurance coverage (Insurance Verification Form) before being able to participate in any club activity. It may be ECU Student Health Insurance or a hospitalization policy carried individually or by the parents.

3. Each club member must complete the Medical History Form before being able to participate in any club activity. All information must be complete, and the form must be screened by a certified member of the Intramural-Recreational Services Sports Medicine Staff. If any questions or problems arise from this history, the sport club member will be referred to a physician before he/she is cleared for participation. All information will be confidential.

4. Each club member must fill out an Information Card. These cards, which include emergency numbers, medical information, and insurance information will be taken to each competition, and will be useful in case of serious injury. Failure of a Sport Club Member to comply with these policies will mean automatic ineligibility for that player until all requirements are completed. A club team that plays an ineligible player runs the risk of losing funding for that sport.

5. Each club member is recommended to have a complete Physical Exam before being able to participate in practices or in competition.

6. Advisors and club officers are responsible for seeing that all forms are signed by club members before participation in club activities.

7. Failure to comply with the above rules will result in appropriate action by the Sport Club Council and Coordinator of Sport Clubs.

8. A file of all forms must be kept by the clubs and a copy given to the Sports Medicine Coordinator.

TRAINER COVERAGE

A qualified trainer is recommended to be present at all sport club practice sessions and competition both on and off campus. This policy shall pertain to any sports club whose program involves strenuous and/or contact activities or other activities where trainer services are warranted.

Trainers are available upon request/based on need from the Coordinator of Sport Clubs and shall be assigned to the various sport clubs. If an Intramural Recreation trainer is not available the clubs are required to assume the responsibility of acquiring the services of a trainer.

The salaries of trainers not provided by IM-REC Services are the sole responsibility of the respective sport club and must be paid from non-allocated funds.

Members of sport clubs shall be able to use the Intramural-Recreational Services training room and trainer services during the scheduled hours as would any ECU student or faculty or staff member.

All appointments for medical physical exams made on campus must be coordinated by the professional Intramural-Recreational Services trainer(s).

EQUIPMENT

Sport clubs, because of the specificity and uniqueness of each particular sport, need certain types of equipment. The responsibility of the equipment for a specific sport lies with the club. Personal equipment, however, must be purchased by individual members of the club. General equipment or equipment that is normally available for use by all students can be checked out at the Intramural-Recreation Equipment Room by presenting the ECU ID card. The following guidelines must be adhered to in relation to sport club equipment.

Purchase

1. All equipment purchased with *allocated* funds becomes the property of East Carolina University and the Department of Intramural-Recreational Services. This equipment is subject to inspection at any time by authorities of the university.
2. The Coordinator of Sport Clubs and the Coordinator of Equipment will assist recognized clubs in the purchase of equipment; however, purchases must be initiated by the individual clubs.
3. Approved equipment expenditures will be charged to the club's allocated budget.

4. Equipment that is not allowed to be purchased with allocated funds can be purchased with club or self-generated funds (nonallocated). This equipment belongs to the club and can be used accordingly.
5. The purchase of equipment must be initiated as far in advance of the date needed as possible and should be done at the beginning of the school year.

EVALUATION

Just as for every other phase of the total Intramural-Recreation program and the university setting, constant evaluation is a necessary part of the sport club program. The sport club program and each club need to be continually evaluated to ensure that the program meets student interest and that it is serving the needs of the participants. The club members, the sport club council, and the coordinator of sport clubs will know through the ongoing process of evaluation how well the clubs are following the guidelines established and how each club can be improved. Evaluation will be done of participation patterns, cost statistics, recurring problem areas, annual reports, budgets, and schedules. Student interest in the club becomes an important factor in the continuation of that club.

CLUB CONDUCT

Upon recognition as a certified Sport Club that club will be permitted to use the name of East Carolina University in affiliation with the respective club title. In using the name of the University the club speaks for the club and club members and *officially* represents both East Carolina University and the Department of Intramural-Recreational Services as a whole. Responsibilities of the club such as carrying on effectively and efficiently the affairs and functions of the club will be performed in accordance to the rules and regulations of East Carolina University and the Department of Intramural-Recreational Services. Club members are expected to conduct themselves in accordance with the University code and act in a mature and responsible manner both *on* and *off* campus.

Failure of any club (or club member) to abide by the rules and regulations or any conduct unbecoming that club and detrimental to the University and Department of Intramural-Recreational Services will be subject to disciplinary action. The disciplinary action taken will depend on the offense committed and may result in loss of club recognition, suspension of club and/or club members, loss of support (monies), or other appropriate action(s) by the Department of Intramural-Recreational Services.

Examples of misconduct are as follows:

1. Use of alcoholic beverages in manner unbecoming a representative of ECU (i.e., public display of drunkenness or inability to participate due to alcohol misuse).
2. Use of drugs including marijuana.
3. Misuse of vehicles (i.e., using vehicles for private concerns, transportation of alcohol and/or drugs, exceeding posted speed limits, interior or exterior vehicle uncleanliness).
4. Damage to ECU or off-campus property, buildings, belongings, and so forth.
5. Public use of profanity and/or profane gestures.
6. Violations of criminal or civil law.

YEARBOOK

Each individual sport club is required to put together a yearbook. This yearbook is considered an explanation and justification of a club's budget request. The yearbook is to be submitted along with the club's budget request to the Coordinator of Sport Clubs and is due two weeks before the last general session meeting of the sport club council. The report will be kept in the sport club office during the following year and will be available on a checkout basis for use as a reference guide. The report can be very useful in promoting the club, recruiting for new members, and justifying the budget request. The yearbook must be in booklet form and must be typewritten. The following items must be included in the report as well as other information deemed pertinent to the interests of each individual club:

1. Goals of the past year—how they were met or how they are currently being met.
2. Goals for the upcoming year—program proposals that will help meet the goals.
3. How does the club benefit the Department of Intramural-Recreational Services, the University, and the student body.
4. A summary report of the past year:
   - Financial
   - Membership and percentage of participation
   - Competition and percentage of participation
   - Exhibitions
   - Problems
5. Pictures of the past year's activities.
6. Publicity and advertising for the past year.
   - Posters

- Flyers
- Articles
- Newsletters
- Advertisements
- Tickets
- Club minutes

7. The club constitution.

All members of the club should take an active part in putting together this yearbook. The yearbook is the personification of the club.

East Carolina University
Department of Intramural-Recreational Services
Request for Sport Club Recognition

I. Name of Club _____ II. Date Submitted _____

III. Representative Petitioning:

Name	Address	Phone
_____	_____	_____

IV. Officers:

Name	Position	Dept./Class	Address	Phone
_____	_____	_____	_____	_____
_____	_____	_____	_____	_____
_____	_____	_____	_____	_____
_____	_____	_____	_____	_____

V. Advisor:

Name	Dept.	Address	Res. Phone	Bus. Phone
_____	_____	_____	_____	_____

VI. Coach:

Name	Dept.	Address	Res. Phone	Bus. Phone
_____	_____	_____	_____	_____

VII. Club Classification:

Competitive _____ Recreational _____ Instructional _____

VIII. Affiliations with Off-Campus Groups (State or National Organizations)

_____   _____

_____   _____

IX. Clubs and/or teams participating in respective sport and with whom scheduling possibilities are available

Club/Team	Institution	Town/State/Zip Code

X. Season of Sport: Fall _____   Spring _____   Summer _____

XI. Purpose and Objective of Club:

A. _____

B. _____

XII. Anticipated number of members: Male _____ Female _____

XIII. Proposed activities for _____ :

A. _____

B. _____

C. _____

D. _____

XIV. Finances:

A. Dues: Yes _____ No _____ Amount: $ _____

B. Campus Fund-Raising Activities (current or proposed):

C. Off-campus Fund-Raising Activities (current or proposed):

D. Current available funds: _____

E. Where are funds banked or deposited? _____

F. Has club or is club receiving financial assistance from a campus source?

Yes _____ No _____

Which source? _____ Amount: _____

G. Has club or is club receiving financial assistance from an off-campus source?

Yes _____   No _____

Which source? _____   Amount: _____

H. Equipment Needs:

_____   _____

_____   _____

I. Facility Needs:

_____   _____

_____   _____

SPORT CLUB COUNCIL USE ONLY

Approved: _____   Date: _____

Disapproved: _____   Date: _____

Reason: _____

Vote results: For _____   Against _____

DEPARTMENTAL USE ONLY

Approved: _____   Date: _____

Disapproved: _____   Date: _____

Reason: _____

By: _____

Coordinator of Sport Clubs
Department of Intramural-Recreational Services

Constitution Submitted: Yes _____   No _____

East Carolina University
Department of Intramural-Recreational Services
Sport Club President's Affidavit

I. I, the undersigned, hereby declare that all members of the _____
_____ Sport Club, East
Carolina University, have fulfilled the following obligations of being a participating member in practices and games.

A. Waiver/Liability Release
B. Insurance Verification
C. Medical History
D. Information Form

II. I will not allow any individual to participate in any practice sessions and/or any type of competition unless the required obligations have been fulfilled.

III. I understand that deviations by any club member from the policies, rules, regulations and procedures as set forth by East Carolina University and the Department of Intramural-Recreational Services will result in disciplinary action by the Sport Club Council and the Coordinator of Sport Clubs.

IV. I hereby authorize, in the name of _____
Sport Club, that the Coordinator of Sport Clubs, Department of Intramural-Recreational Services be allowed to:

A. Administer allocated funds.
B. Receive reports of nonallocated funds/accounts.
C. Administer the purchase and maintenance of all equipment purchased with allocated funds.
D. Receive reports of nonallocated equipment purchases.
E. Receive reports of all financial transactions.
F. Receive reports of all club meetings, activities, and events.

President Signature _____ Date _____

Advisor Signature _____ Date _____

Department of Intramural-Recreational Services
East Carolina University
Medical History

Complete form in ink only.

Name _____ Age _____ Sex _____

Campus Address _____

Campus Phone _____ Height _____ Weight _____

Birth Date: _____ Sport(s) _____

_____

_____

Parent's Name _____ Phone _____

Parents' Address _____
                 Street   City   State   Zip Code

Who shall we notify in event of an emergency?

Name _____ Phone _____
                                              Business   Home

Address _____
         Street   City   State   Zip Code

This information will be kept confidential.

Circle the appropriate answer:

Diseases and Illnesses

Yes No   1. Have you ever experienced an epileptic seizure or been informed that you
             might have epilepsy?

Yes No   2. Have you ever had hepatitis?

Yes No   3. Have you been treated for infectious mononucleosis, virus pneumonia, or
             any other infectious disease during the past 12 months?

Yes No   4. Have you ever been treated for diabetes? If so do you take medication or shots?

Yes No   5. Have you ever been treated or informed by a medical doctor that you have
             had scarlet fever?

Yes No   6. Have you ever been treated or informed by a medical doctor that you have
             had rheumatic fever?

Yes No   7. Have you ever been told that you have a heart murmur? If so do you take
             medication?   Medication _____

Yes No   8. Do you have any known allergies? If so, do you take medication?

             Allergic to _____

             Medication _____

Yes No   9. Do you have any known allergies to drugs (such as penicillin)? If so, to what?

             _____

Yes No 10. Have you ever been "knocked-out" or experienced a concussion?

Yes   No   11. If answer to question 10 is yes, have you been "knocked-out" more than once?

Yes   No   12. If answers to questions 10 and 11 are yes, did the attending physician have you stay overnight in a hospital?

Eyes and Dental

Yes   No   13. Do you wear eyeglasses?

Yes   No   14. Do you wear contact lenses?

Yes   No   15. If answer to above is yes, do you wear them during athletic participation?

Yes   No   16. Do you wear any dental appliance? If answer is yes, underscore appropriate appliance: permanent bridge, permanent crown or jacket, removable partial or full plate.

Bone and Joint

Yes   No   17. Have you ever been treated for Osgood-Schlatter disease?

Yes   No   18. Have you ever been treated for calcium deposits? If so, give location. __

_____

Yes   No   19. Have you ever had any injury to the neck involving nerves, vertebrae, or vertebral discs?

Yes   No   20. Have you ever had a shoulder dislocation, separation, or other injury that incapacitated you for a week or longer?

Yes   No   21. Have you ever been advised to have surgery to correct a shoulder condition?

Yes   No   22. If answer to question 21 is yes, did you seek the advice or care of a medical doctor?   If so, when? _____

Yes   No   23. Have you ever experienced an injury to your arms, elbows, or shoulders?

Yes   No   24. Have you ever had an injury to your back?

Yes   No   25. If answer to question 24 is yes, did you seek the advice or care of a medical doctor?

Yes   No   26. Do you experience pain in the back? If answer is yes, indicate frequency with which you experience pain by underscoring answer: very seldom, occasionally, frequently, only after vigorous exercise or heavy lifting.

Yes   No   27. Do you think your back is weak?

Yes   No   28. Have you ever been told that you injured the ligaments of either knee joint?

Yes   No   29. Have you ever been told that you injured the cartilage of either knee joint?

Yes   No   30. Have you ever been advised to have surgery to a knee to correct a condition?

Yes   No   31. If answer to question 30 is yes, has the surgery been completed?

Yes   No   32. Have you ever experienced a severe sprain of either ankle?

Yes   No   33. Do you have a pin, screw, or plate somewhere in your body as a result of a bone or joint surgery? If answer is yes, indicate anatomical site and date of surgery. _____

_____

Yes   No   34. Have you had a fracture during the past 2 years? If answer is yes, indicate site of fracture. _____

_____

General

Yes   No   35. Have you ever been told that you have a hernia?

Yes   No   36. If answer to the above question is yes, has the hernia been surgically repaired?

Yes   No   37. Have you had any operation during the past 2 years? If answer is yes, indicate anatomical site of operation and date. _____

_____

Yes   No   38. Have you had any additional illnesses, injuries or operations? (other than childhood diseases). If answer is yes, indicate specific illness or operation.

_____

_____

Yes   No   39. Have you ever experienced heat exhaustion and/or heat stroke? If so, when?

_____

Yes   No   40. Have you ever had blood in your urine or had kidney or urinary problems?

41. Name your family physician and give his or her address:

Name: _____

Address: _____

All of the above questions have been answered completely and truthfully to the best of my knowledge.

Please give date of last tetanus shot. _____

_____

Signature

_____

Date

Notes:

East Carolina University
Department of Intramural-Recreational Sports
Sport Club Contract for Officials/Judges

I. A. Name of Official: _____

  B. Address: _____

  C. Town/State/Zip Code:

        _____

  D. Phone: (_____) _____-_____

  E. Social Security #: _____

II. Certification: A. _____

          B. _____

III. A. I, _____ , hereby agree to
officiate/judge the following East Carolina University _____
Sport Club games for $ _____ per game.

  B. 1. Date(s) _____ _____ _____ _____ _____ _____

      2. Day(s) _____ _____ _____ _____ _____ _____

      3. Time(s) _____ _____ _____ _____ _____ _____

      4. Location _____ _____ _____ _____ _____ _____

  C. Signed: _____ Date: _____

IV. ECU _____ Sport Club Representative:

  Signed _____

FOR DEPARTMENTAL USE ONLY:

Approved: _____ Date: _____

Disapproved: _____ Date: _____

Reason: _____

_____

By: _____
    Coordinator of Sport Clubs
    Department of Intramural-Recreational Services
    East Carolina University

East Carolina University
Department of Intramural-Recreational Services
Sport Club Trip Application
(Application must be filed 10 working days before date of trip)

I. Club: _____   Date: _____ , 19 _____

II. Purpose: _____

III. Destination: _____

IV. A. Departure: Day/Date _____   Hours _____

    B. Return: Day/Date _____   Hour _____

V. A. Advisor accompanying club:

Name	Dept.	Campus Address	Campus Phone

    B. Coach accompanying club:

Name	Dept.	Campus Address	Campus Phone

    C. Trainer accompanying club:

Name	Dept.	Campus Address	Campus Phone

VI. If overnight trip list information for club location:

Residence Unit	Address	Phone	Day/Date

VII. Method of Transportation:

    A. University Vehicle(s) _____   Private Vehicle(s) _____

    Other (explain) _____

    B. If by private vehicle list for each driver

Name	Address	Phone	Make of car/year	Insurance Co. Policy No.

VIII. On an accompanying sheet of paper list the names of *all* club members going on the trip. The application will not be approved without a complete listing. Members who have not completed all requirements for practice or competition will not be approved (waiver, insurance, information card, history). If classes are to be missed the Dean of Students must grant approval.

Submitted by: _____   _____
              Signature Club President   Date

              _____   _____
              Signature Club Advisor   Date

_____

DEPARTMENTAL USE ONLY

Approved (   )   Disapproved (   )   Date: _____

Reason: _____

By: _____
    Coordinator of Sport Clubs, IRS

Sport Club Constitution

In the Matthews survey of 1982 (see chapter 16), 83% of the schools surveyed required sport clubs to file a constitution with a designated office. The two most common items demanded were a list of elected officers and a list of all club members.

The constitution for a sport club is the instrument that provides the guidelines by which the club members will operate their club. This document describes the parameters within which the activities of the club take place.

A constitution sets up the club as a distinct entity, making it quite different from the other organizations. This written document enables the university and college administrators to distinguish one club from another, especially when several clubs are organized around one sport. For example, in the martial arts there is more than one type of karate. Therefore, distinction must be made as to what type of karate is being sponsored by the club, thus pointing up the differences from the other karate clubs. The continuity and operational framework provided by the constitution make it much easier for the clubs to exist from year to year.

The sample given here was chosen from approximately 100 that were sent to the author. It is typical of those submitted, yet more comprehensive than most.

THE PENNSYLVANIA STATE UNIVERSITY
NITTANY DIVERS
CONSTITUTION

Article I: Name

The name of this organization shall be The Pennsylvania State University Nittany Divers, hereafter referred to as Nittany Divers.

Article II: Purposes

The purposes of this organization are as follows:

A. To provide a common meeting ground for all students interested in any phase of skin or scuba diving.
B. To encourage, promote, and aid in any way possible the study of the underwater world, including oceanography, marine biology, limnology, ichthyology, and speleology.
C. To assume sponsorship of social and sporting events among persons interested in skin and scuba diving.
D. To serve as a clearing house for diving information, and to actively promote programs along the lines of safety and research.
E. To promote and encourage skin and scuba diving in a safe and sane manner and to aid in the instruction in the proper use of skin and scuba diving equipment.
F. To promote sportsmanship, competition, and good fellowship among its members.

Article III: Membership

A. Regular membership in Nittany Divers shall be open to all interested persons.
   1. Yearly dues will be set up by the Executive Committee.
   2. Members must have paid the membership fee as determined by the Executive Committee.
B. Each regular member of the Nittany Divers shall receive a membership card upon payment of the membership fee. This card will entitle the member to participate in all functions of the club and in all events sponsored or arranged by the club.
   1. Participation in club dives requires a certification card issued by a nationally recognized certifying organization (PADI).

C. Honorary membership in Nittany Divers shall be granted by a majority of the quorum.

   1. All past officers are entitled to honorary membership.

D. Though every precaution will be taken to ensure the safety of members, the Nittany Divers cannot accept any responsibility whatsoever for personal loss or injury.

E. Any member may be excluded from club activities by the vote of a majority of the quorum if they find that the member is disregarding the rules of the club.

Article IV: Finances

All funds belonging to the club will be placed on deposit with and handled through the Associated Student Activities (ASA) in accordance with rules and procedures established by the ASA.

Article V: Organization

The governing body of the club shall be the Executive Committee, which will consist of the President, the Vice President, the Secretary, and the Treasurer, who will work in conjunction with the faculty advisor(s), who is/are ad hoc.

Article VI: Advisor

The duties of the advisor will be as noted in the *Guide to University Regulation Concerning Student Affairs, Conduct and Discipline*.

Article VII: Elections

A. The outgoing President will conduct nominations for each of the four officers on the Executive Committee by the present club members.

   1. Elections will be held at the following club meeting, not to be held less than one week or more than one month following the nominations.

B. Candidates for the four offices of the Executive Committee shall be elected from the regular membership by a majority vote, a quorum being present.

C. The candidates for the Executive Committee must be currently enrolled in the University as full-time undergraduate or graduate students.

1. The candidates for the office of President shall have at least fourth-term standing as an undergraduate and shall have been a regular member of the club for at least two terms before the election.

D. The terms of office for members of the Executive Committee shall run for one year, commencing with the first regular meeting after elections in January and running until the first meeting after the election in January the following year.

Article VIII: Meetings

A. Regular meetings shall be held at least twice a term during the fall, winter, and spring terms. The time, place, and date for these meetings shall be set by the President. The first regular meeting of the school year shall be held no later than the end of the first month of classes in the fall term.
B. Additional meetings shall be held at the discretion of the Executive Committee.
C. A quorum shall consist of at least 25 active members.
   1. Before a vote is taken, the Secretary shall count the number of persons present and announce whether or not a quorum is present.
   2. Regular members shall be defined as those paid-up members whose names appeared in the Secretary's records at the beginning of the meeting.
D. All regular and special meetings shall be conducted in accord with Robert's Rules of Order.

Article IX: Removal From Office

A. Any officer of Nittany Divers who shall be guilty of misconduct in office may, at any regular meeting of the club, be reprimanded or removed from office, as the members shall determine, but the accusation shall be in writing and shall state the offense. The written accusation shall be signed by at least ten regular members of the club and shall be on the table for consideration at least 14 days before the meeting when a forum shall take place. A negative vote shall require two-thirds majority of the members present (there being a quorum present), but a simple majority vote may decide the penalty.
B. Any officer shall be automatically removed from office if placed on probation by the University.
C. Any officer shall resign upon leaving the University.
D. Any vacated office shall be filled by an Executive Committee nomination, followed by club approval.

Article X: Referendum

Upon receipt of written requests from a member submitted at least 14 days before the meeting, the club shall be required to conduct a vote upon a given subject at the next meeting. This procedure shall not be applicable to removal of officers or amendments to the Constitution and Bylaws.

Article XI: Amendments

A. Any proposed amendment shall be automatically tabled until the meeting following that at which it was first presented, then read, discussed, and voted upon.
B. An amendment to the Constitution shall require the affirmative vote of two thirds of the quorum.

Article XII: Bylaws

The Constitution shall be supplemented by a set of bylaws. These shall define the rights, privileges, and obligations of club members.

Article XIII: Ratification

A. This Constitution shall be in effect when ratified by two thirds of the members present at the meeting when presented for ratification, there being a quorum present.
B. This Constitution shall not be considered retroactive in any way.

NITTANY DIVERS
BYLAWS

Article I: Duties of the Executive Committee and the Club Officers

I. The Executive Committee shall:
   A. Appoint chairpersons of any standing committee.
   B. Meet at least twice a term at such a time as to follow the regular or additional meetings of the club.
   C. Assume all powers and responsibilities delegated to it by the club membership.
   D. Be called together by the President of the Nittany Divers.

II. Duties of the officers:
  A. The President of Nittany Divers shall:
    1. Preside over the meetings of Nittany Divers while they are in session.
    2. Preside over the Executive Committee while it is in session.
    3. Appoint temporary committees and chairpersons thereof.
    4. Assume all additional powers and responsibilities delegated to him or her by the membership.
  B. The Vice President of Nittany Divers shall:
    1. Assume the duties of the President in his or her absence.
    2. Act as assistant to the President in his or her regular duties.
    3. Assume such additional powers and responsibilities delegated to him or her by the membership.
  C. The Secretary of Nittany Divers shall:
    1. Keep minutes of all meetings.
    2. Transcribe the minutes into a permanent record after they have been adopted.
    3. Keep the membership roll in good order.
    4. Notify members of all meetings.
    5. Answer any inquiries or other mail and carry on such correspondence as deemed necessary by the President.
    6. Keep a permanent record of all students registered in Nittany Divers courses.
    7. Keep a record of instructors' contracts.
    8. A copy of course records shall be kept on file at the office of the Director of Aquatics at the University.
    9. Assume additional duties as delegated by the membership.
  D. The Treasurer of Nittany Divers shall:
    1. Be responsible for collecting all dues and course fees.
    2. Be responsible for paying club-incurred debts and instructor fees.
    3. Maintain records of money transactions involving:
      a. Equipment purchases, rental and sales.
      b. Fees from membership and courses.
      c. Special projects.
    4. Present treasurer's report at the beginning of each club meeting.
    5. Assume additional duties delegated by the membership.

Article II: Committees

  I. Standing committees may be established by a majority vote of the members, there being a quorum present.

II. Temporary committees shall be appointed by the President with the approval of the Executive Committee whenever the need for such committees shall arise.

Article III: Conditions for a Club-Sponsored Dive

 I. Advisor's knowledge of the planned dive.
 II. All club members participating in the dive must be certified divers, or if uncertified divers wish to participate, the diver(s) must be accompanied by a certified instructor.
 III. A dive master shall be appointed by the Executive Committee for each club-sponsored dive.

Article IV: Nominations and Elections

 I. Nominations
   A. Candidates for the Executive Committee shall be nominated by the members of Nittany Divers.
   B. Each nomination shall be accompanied by the consent of the candidate.
   C. Nominations shall be held in accordance with Article VII, Section A of the Constitution.
 II. Elections
   A. The election of the Executive Committee will take place at the regularly scheduled meeting in January of each year.
   B. The Executive Committee shall be elected in the order of President, Vice President, Secretary and Treasurer, with the candidates for each office eligible for each remaining office on a write-in ballot.

Article V: Courses of Nittany Divers

 I. When possible, the club may offer scuba courses to the University family.
 II. Instructors shall be contracted in writing by the Executive Committee and are subject to approval by the Executive Committee.
 III. The contract shall include a minimum number of students allowed in the course and the instructor's fee. A copy of the current contract is to be placed with the Bylaws for examination by any member if wanted or needed. Course fees shall be decided by the Executive Committee.

Article VI: Adoption of the Bylaws

I. The Bylaws will become effective immediately upon adoption by a two-thirds majority of the members present at a regularly scheduled meeting, there being a quorum present.

Article VII: Amendments to the Bylaws

I. Any amendment to the Bylaws must be passed by a two-thirds vote of the members at a regularly scheduled meeting, there being a quorum present.
II. All proposed amendments must be tabled until one meeting after their first presentation before they may be discussed and voted upon.

Matthews' Sport Club Administration Questionnaire, 1982

As indicated in part V, Surveys, this questionnaire was sent to directors of campus recreation at 299 institutions of higher education. The results tabulated from the returned questionnaires served as the basis of comparison with the data secured by Phelps' 1969 survey.

THE ADMINISTRATION OF SPORT CLUBS DIRECTORS' QUESTIONNAIRE

Please circle one response for each question unless otherwise instructed.

I. Philosophy

Please circle the degree of your agreement or disagreement with the following statements.

	Strongly agree	Agree	Neither agree nor disagree (uncommitted)	Disagree	Strongly disagree
1. The sport club program should be student directed.	1	2	3	4	5
2. Sport clubs, particularly the team sports, are a good source of new intercollegiate sports.	1	2	3	4	5
3. Many of the existing sports clubs (e.g., badminton) generate the majority of their matches and competition on an *intra*club basis.	1	2	3	4	5
4. Each registered sport club should be given a specific financial appropriation per year to run its own program.	1	2	3	4	5
5. A sport club competing on an intercollegiate basis is generally administratively feasible.	1	2	3	4	5
6. The sport club program is a part of the total intramural program.	1	2	3	4	5
7. The Intramural Department should *not* be involved with the sport club program.	1	2	3	4	5
8. Whenever possible, sport clubs are assisted in making the transition to intercollegiate athletics.	1	2	3	4	5

9. Comments: _____

_____

II. Registration and Institutional Sanction

10a. Are sport clubs officially recognized by the President of the Institution, Board of Regents, or Board of Directors?

Yes   1

No   2

10b. Are sport clubs officially recognized by other administrators within the institution?

Yes   1

No   2

11a. Is there a person in the institution designated as the coordinator or a liaison for the sport club program?

Yes   1

No (*Skip to question 12*)   2

11b. Please indicate his or her title, rank, and department.

_____

_____

12. Which department(s) within the institution is (are) responsible for the administration of the sport club program? (*Circle all that apply*)

   a. Intercollegiate Athletics   1

   b. Intramurals   2

   c. Military (ROTC)   3

   d. Office of Student Affairs   4

   e. Physical Education   5

   f. Recreation   1

   g. Student Union   2

   h. Student Senate   3

   i. Student Finance Committee   4

   j. Other (*Specify*) _____   5

13. Is each sport club required to file the following with the administering department or the office of student affairs?

	Yes	No
a. Written constitution	1	2
b. List of elected officers	1	2
c. List of all club members	1	2

14a. Does each sport club have an advisor?

    Yes   1

    No (*Skip to question 15*)   2

14b. Is the advisor selected by the club members?

    Yes (*Skip to question 14d*)   1

    No   2

14c. If the advisor is appointed, by whom? (*Circle all that apply*)

    (1) Director of Athletics   1

    (2) Director of Intramurals   2

    (3) Administering department   3

    (4) Department chair   4

    (5) Interested faculty professor   5

    (6) Other _____   6

14d. Is the advisor a member of the institution's faculty?

    Yes   1

    No (*Skip to question 15*)   2

14e. Is the advisor usually a member of the faculty of the administering department?

    Yes   1

    No   2

15. May a registered sport club in good standing officially use the name of the institution as a part of the recognized name of the club? (e.g., Indiana University Rugby Club)

    Yes   1

    No   2

16. May official recognition of a sport club be withdrawn for violation of institutional regulations?

    Yes   1

    No   2

17a. Does your institution have a sport club council?

    Yes   1

    No (*Skip to question 18*)   2

17b. Please indicate the council's function(s): (*Circle all that apply*)

    (1) Establish policies   1

(2) Revise general regulations pertaining
    to all sport clubs   2

(3) Serve as a liaison between sport clubs
    and coordinator of the program   3

(4) Schedule activities   4

(5) Determine budget   5

(6) Evaluate program   6

(7) Others _____ 7

18. Comments: _____

    _____

    _____

19. For each of the sport clubs listed, please indicate the following:

Sport clubs	a. If the club was active in fiscal year 1981-1982	b. If the club competed on an interclub basis	c. If the club was corecreational (men and women)	d. The approximate membership for 1981-1982)
(1) Archery	1	2	3	_____
(2) Badminton	1	2	3	_____
(3) Basketball	1	2	3	_____
(4) Bowling	1	2	3	_____
(5) Canoeing	1	2	3	_____
(6) Cricket	1	2	3	_____
(7) Curling	1	2	3	_____
(8) Cycling	1	2	3	_____
(9) Fencing	1	2	3	_____
(10) Football, touch	1	2	3	_____
(11) Gymnastics	1	2	3	_____
(12) Handball	1	2	3	_____
(13) Horseback riding	1	2	3	_____
(14) Ice hockey	1	2	3	_____
(15) Judo	1	2	3	_____
(16) Karate	1	2	3	_____
(17) Lacrosse	1	2	3	_____
(18) Modern dance	1	2	3	_____

(19) Racquetball	1	2	3	_____
(20) Pistol shooting	1	2	3	_____
(21) Polo, horse	1	2	3	_____
(22) Riflery	1	2	3	_____
(23) Rodeo	1	2	3	_____
(24) Rowing	1	2	3	_____
(25) Rugby	1	2	3	_____
(26) Sailing	1	2	3	_____
(27) Scuba diving	1	2	3	_____
(28) Skiing, snow	1	2	3	_____
(29) Skiing, water	1	2	3	_____
(30) Skydiving	1	2	3	_____
(31) Soaring	1	2	3	_____
(32) Soccer	1	2	3	_____
(33) Softball	1	2	3	_____
(34) Square dance	1	2	3	_____
(35) Squash	1	2	3	_____
(36) Swimming	1	2	3	_____
(37) Table tennis	1	2	3	_____
(38) Tennis	1	2	3	_____
(39) Track and field	1	2	3	_____
(40) Volleyball	1	2	3	_____
(41) Water polo	1	2	3	_____
(42) Weight lifting	1	2	3	_____
(43) Wrestling	1	2	3	_____
(44) Others _____	1	2	3	_____

III. Eligibility

20. Are the following individuals eligible for sport club membership?

	Yes	No
a. Undergraduate students	1	2
b. Graduate students	1	2
c. Faculty members	1	2
d. Nonacademic staff	1	2

e. Alumni   1   2

f. Others (*Specify*) _____   1   2

21a. Are there specific scholastic requirements for sport club membership?

Yes   1

No (*Skip to question 22*)   2

21b. Are the requirements as stringent as those utilized by the National Collegiate Athletic Association?

Yes   1

No   2

22a. Are sport club members eligible for intramural competition in the sport represented by the club?

Yes   1

No (*Skip to question 23*)   2

22b. Is there a limit as to the number of club members on the same team?

Yes   1

No   2

23. Are members of aquatic activity clubs required to pass a basic swimming test?

Yes   1

No   2

IV. Finance

24a. Do sport club members pay dues?

Yes   1

No (*Skip to question 25*)   2

24b. If dues are paid, what are the (1) minimum and (2) maximum yearly (two semesters) assessments?

	1. Minimum assessment	2. Maximum assessment
$2.00 or less	1	1
$2.01 to $4.00	2	2
$4.01 to $6.00	3	3
$6.01 to $8.00	4	4
$8.01 to $10.00	5	5

$10.01 to $20.00	6	6
$20.01 to $30.00	7	7
$30.01 to $40.00	8	8
$40.01 to more	9	9
Depends on budgetary needs	10	10

25. Is the sport club program partially financed by

	Yes	No
a. general student fee?	1	2
b. budget of administering department?	1	2
c. gate receipts of club contests?	1	2
d. fund-raising projects?	1	2
e. commercial grants?	1	2
f. gifts?	1	2

26a. Do sport clubs have advisors?

Yes   1

No (*Skip to question 27*)   2

26b. Are club advisors paid for their services?

Yes   1

No (*Skip to question 26d*)   2

26c. What is the approximate hourly remuneration?

$3.50 or less   1

$3.51 to $4.50   2

$4.51 to $6.00   3

$6.01 to $8.00   4

$8.01 to $10.00   5

$10.01 or more   6

26d. Are club advisors given a decreased teaching, administrative, and coaching load?

Yes   1

No (*Skip to question 27*)   2

26e. What is the percent *decrease* in the teaching, administrative, and coaching load?

_____%

27a. Are nonuniversity personnel utilized to give lessons to the sports club members?

Yes   1

No (*Skip to question 28*)   2

27b. Are these nonuniversity persons paid by the club for their services?

Yes   1

No   2

28a. Is the sport club treasurer required to keep a record of all business transactions?

Yes   1

No (*Skip to question 28c*)   2

28b. Are these financial records subject to audit by institutional officials?

Yes   1

No   2

28c. Is the treasurer required to receive the advisor's approval or signature before writing a pay voucher?

Yes   1

No   2

29. Does the institution accept the financial responsibility for individual club debts?

Yes   1

No   2

30. What was the total 1981-82 fiscal year sport club program operating budget, excluding use of the facilities, as subsidized by the institution?

$ _____

V. Medical Supervision

	Yes	No
31a. Are all members of the contact sport clubs required to have the results of a recent physical examination on file with the Student Health Service?	1	2
31b. Are members of sport clubs required to sign an accident liability release form?	3	4
31c. Are parents or guardians, of club members under 21 years of age required to sign a consent and release form?	1	2

31d. Is an injury report form available to record all injuries resulting from participation in sport club activities?   3   4

31e. Is medical treatment provided at the Student Health Service for injuries resulting from sport club practice sessions and contests?   1   2

31f. Is a student athletic trainer present at all interclub home contests involving contact sports?   1   2

31g. Is a student athletic trainer present at all practice sessions involving contact sports?   3   4

31h. Is an athletic trainer present at all interclub home contests involving contact sports?   1   2

31i. Is an athletic trainer present at all practice sessions involving contact sports?   3   4

31j. Is a physician present at all interclub home contests involving contact sports?   1   2

31k. Is a physician present at all practice sessions involving contact sports?   3   4

31l. Is the institution financially responsible for injuries resulting from sport club practice sessions and contests?   1   2

31m. Does the institution subscribe to liability insurance to protect employees and club advisors against suits invoked for injuries occurring during practice sessions or contests?   3   4

31n. Is a medical examination required before a player is permitted to return to the activity following illness or injury?   1   2

32a. Is student health insurance available to members of sport clubs?

Yes   1

No (*Skip to question 33*)   2

32b. Is it mandatory?

Yes   1

No   2

VI. Equipment and Facilities

33. Do club members provide all of their own personal equipment?

    Yes   1

    No   2

34. Does your institution furnish the following supplementary equipment? (*Circle all that apply*)

    a. Ammunition   1

    b. Archery equipment   2

    c. Balls   3

    d. Bats   4

    e. Paddles and racquets   5

    f. Shoes, cleated   1

    g. Shoes, tennis   2

    h. Skis   3

    i. Shuttlecocks   4

    j. Uniforms, practice   5

    k. Uniforms, game   1

    l. Others (*Specify*) _____   2

35. Does your institution provide a capital outlay for initial and basic equipment for club use? (e.g., kayak)

    Yes   1

    No   2

36. Are facilities owned and operated by the institution available for club use?

    Yes   1

    No (*Skip to question 37*) 2

36a. Are they all provided free of charge?

    Yes   1

    No (*Skip to question 37*) 2

36b. Circle those requiring a nominal fee:

    (1) Archery range   1

    (2) Bowling lane   2

    (3) Dance studio   3

    (4) Diamonds, softball   4

(5)	Fencing room	5
(6)	Fields, play	1
(7)	Golf course	2
(8)	Gymnasium	3
(9)	Gymnastics room	4
(10)	Handball and racquetball courts	5
(11)	Hiking trails	1
(12)	Ice-skating arena	2
(13)	Lakes, reservoirs, rivers	3
(14)	Outdoor nature center	4
(15)	Rifle range	5
(16)	Roller skating arena	1
(17)	Ski and toboggan slope	2
(18)	Squash courts	3
(19)	Swimming and diving pool	4
(20)	Tennis courts	5
(21)	Weight room	1
(22)	Wrestling room	2

37a. Are locker spaces available for club members?

Yes 1

No (*Skip to question 38*) 2

37b. Are locker spaces provided free of charge?

Yes 1

No 2

37c. Is a towel service provided free of charge?

Yes 1

No 2

VII. Interclub Competition

38. Do sport clubs engage in interclub competition?

Yes 1

No 2

39. Which of the following are sources of competition for your sport club teams? (*Circle all that apply*)

   a. Other sport club teams   1

   b. Intercollegiate teams   2

   c. YMCA teams   3

   d. AAU teams   4

   e. Sports Days   5

   f. Other (*Specify*) _____   6

   _____

40. Does your institution permit sport clubs to establish conference or league affiliations?

   Yes   1
   No   2

41a. Does an administrator give final approval to all sport club competitive schedules?

   Yes   1

   No (*Skip to question 42*)   2

41b. Who gives final approval to all sport club competitive schedules? (*Circle all that apply*)

   (1) Director of Athletics   1

   (2) Director of Intramurals   2

   (3) Chair of Department of Physical   3
        Education

   (4) Student Activities Office   4

   (5) Others (*Specify*) _____   5

41c. Are these schedules limited as to number of games per season?

   Yes   1

   No   2

42 Does the administering department assume the total expenses incurred for interclub competition, including

	Yes	No	If "no," what percent of the expenses does it assume?
(1) game equipment?	1	2	_____%

(2) game officials?   3   4   _____%

(3) lodging for visiting team   1   2   _____%
members?

(4) meals for visiting team?   3   4   _____%

(5) portable bleachers, erec-   1   2   _____%
tion and removal?

(6) public address system,   3   4   _____%
installation, operation,
and removal?

(7) use of facility?   1   2   _____%

		Yes	No
43.	Are sport clubs permitted to charge admission to their interclub contests?	1	2
44.	Do sport clubs derive income from concessions sold at interclub contests?	3	4
45.	Are local news media permitted to use such terms as "varsity," "returning lettermen," and "J-V team," when referring to sport club teams?	1	2

VIII. Travel

46. Do teams travel for interclub competition?

Yes   1
No (*skip to question 52*)   2

47a. Is team travel for interclub competition restricted during the regular season?

Yes   1

No (*Skip to question 49*)   2

47b. What is the maximum *radius* of travel allowed?

1-100 miles   1

101-150 miles   2

151-200 miles   3

201-250 miles   4

251-300 miles   5

301-400 miles   6

401-500 miles   7

501-1,000 miles   8

1,001 or more   9

48a. Does an administrator give the final approval to sport club travel requests?

Yes   1

No (*Skip to question 50*)   2

48b. Who gives final approval to travel requests? (*Circle all that apply*)

(1) Director of Athletics   1

(2) Director of Intramurals   2

(3) Chair of Department of Physical   3
Education

(4) Sport Club Coordinator   4

(5) Student Activities Office   5

(6) Dean of Students   1

(7) Others (*Specify*) _____   2

49a. Who provides the vehicle for off-campus competition? (*Circle all that apply*)

(1) Public Carrier   1

(2) Student   2

(3) Institution   3

49b. If "student" provides the vehicle, is he or she required to have a minimum bodily injury liability (e.g., $25,000 each person and $50,000 each occurrence) and property damage liability (e.g., $10,000 each occurrence) automobile insurance coverage?

Yes   1

No   2

	Yes	No
50a. Are sport club members given an expense allowance for lodging expenses on overnight trips?	1	2
50b. Are sport club members given an expense allowance for meals en route to and from contests?	3	4
50c. Is the advisor required to make all trips with the club?	1	2
50d. May another approved adult substitute for the advisor on trips?	3	4

50e. Are coed club members permitted to travel with   1   2
the club team?

50f. Is interclub competition scheduled only on week-   3   4
ends (Friday evening, Saturday, Sunday)?

50g. Do members of the sport club traveling team   1   2
receive excused absences for classes missed dur-
ing trips away from the campus for interclub
competition?

Directory of Allied Sport Associations in the United States and Canada

Part I of this directory lists fifty-six general organizations related to sport and is organized into the following groups: education, equipment, fitness, gymnastics, handicapped, military, Olympic development, recreation, sport medicine, and youth development.

Part II, Specific Sport Organzations, lists in alphabetical order those groups or agencies which are directly related to a specific sport. They run the gamut from archery to wrestling, with a total of 124 listed.

PART I-GENERAL ORGANIZATIONS RELATED TO SPORT

Education

American Alliance for Health, Physical Education, Recreation, and Dance
1900 Association Drive
Reston, VA 22091

American Association for Leisure and Recreation
1900 Association Drive
Reston, VA 22091

American Sports Education Institute/Boosters Club of America
200 N. Castlewood Drive
North Palm Beach, FL 33408

Athletic Institute
200 N. Castlewood Drive
North Palm Beach, FL 33408

Canadian Association for Health, Physical Education/Recreation
333 River Road
Ottawa, Ontario, Canada K1L 8H9

Canadian Colleges Athletic Association
333 River Road
Ottawa, Ontario, Canada K1L 8H9

Canadian Intramural Recreation Association
333 River Road
Ottawa, Ontario, Canada K1L 8H9

Canadian School Sport Federation
Colonel Gray High School
Charlottetown, Prince Edward Island, Canada C1A 4S6

College Sports Information Directors of America
Box 114, Texas A&I University
Kingsville, TX 78363

Intercollegiate Association of Amateur Athletes of America
P.O. Box 3
Centerville, MA 02632

International Collegiate Sports Foundation, Inc.
P.O. Box 866
Plano, TX 75074

National Association of Collegiate Directors of Athletics
1229 Smith Court, Box 16428
Cleveland, OH 44116

National Association for Girls and Women in Sports
1900 Association Drive
Reston, VA 22091

National Association for Sport and Physical Education
1900 Association Drive
Reston, VA 22091

National Association of Intercollegiate Athletics
1221 Baltimore Avenue
Kansas City, MO 64105

National Collegiate Athletic Association
P.O. Box 1906
Mission, KS 66201

National Federation of High School Directors of Athletics
P.O. Box 20626
Kansas City, MO 64195

National Intramural-Recreation Sports Association
Dixon Recreation Center
Oregon State University
Corvallis, OR 97331

National Junior College Athletic Association
12 E. 2nd Street
Hutchinson, KS 67504

National Youth Sports Coaches Association
2611 Old Okeechobee Road
West Palm Beach, FL 33409

U.S. Collegiate Sports Council
University of South Carolina
Blatt PE Center
Columbia, SC 29208

Women's Sports Foundation
342 Madison Avenue
Suite 728
New York, New York 10173

Equipment

Athletic Equipment Managers Association
723 Kiel Court
Bowling Green, OH 43402

Fitness

Aerobic and Fitness Association of America
15250 Ventura Blvd., Suite 802
Sherman Oaks, CA 91403

American Running and Fitness Association
2420 K Street NW
Washington, DC 20037

Association for Fitness in Business
1312 Washington Boulevard
Stamford, CT 06902

Association of Physical Fitness Centers
5272 River Road, Suite 500
Bethesda, MD 20816

National Spa and Pool Institute
2111 Eisenhower Avenue
Alexandria, VA 22314

National Strength and Conditioning Association
P.O. Box 81410
Lincoln, NE 68501

President's Council on Physical Fitness and Sports
450 5th Street NW #7103
Washington, DC 20001

Gymnastics

U.S. Gymnastics Federation
200 S. Capitol Avenue
Suite 110
Indianapolis, IN 46225

Handicapped

American Athletic Association of the Deaf
3916 Lantern Drive
Silver Spring, MD 20902

National Wheelchair Athletic Association
2107 Templeton Gap Road
Suite C
Colorado Springs, CO 80907

National Wheelchair Basketball Association
110 Seaton Building—University of Kentucky
Lexington, KY 40506

Special Olympics, Inc.
1350 New York Avenue
Suite 500, N.W.
Washington, DC 20005

U.S. Association for Blind Athletes
55 W. California Avenue
Beach Haven Pack, NJ 08008

Military

Army Sports (Physical Activity Division)
HODA, DAAG-MSP
Alexandria, VA 22331

Olympic Development

Amateur Athletic Union AAU House
3400 W. 86th Street
Indianapolis, IN 46268

Athletics Congress of the USA
200 South Capitol Avenue
Suite 140
Indianapolis, IN 46225

International Sports Exchange
5982 Mia Court
Plainfield, IN 46168

United States Olympic Committee
1750 E. Boulder Street
Colorado Springs, CO 80909

Recreation

Council of Park and Recreation Consultants
100 Arrival Avenue
Ronkonkoma, NY 11779

National Association of Sports Officials
1700 N. Main Street, 2nd Floor
Racine, WI 53402

National Institute on Parks and Ground Management
P.O. Box 1936
Appleton, WI 54913

National Recreation and Park Association
3101 Park Ctr. Drive, 12th Floor
Alexandria, VA 22302

National Senior Sports Association
317 Cameron Street
Alexandria, VA 22314

Sports Medicine

American Athletic Trainers Association and Certification Board
660 W. Duarte Road
Arcadia, CA 91006

American College of Sports Medicine
P.O. Box 1440
Indianapolis, IN 46206

American Medical Association
535 North Dearborn Street
Chicago, IL 60610

American Orthopaedic Society for Sports Medicine
70 West Hubbard Street
Chicago, IL 60610

American Osteopathic Academy of Sports Medicine
1551 NW 54th, Suite 200
Seattle, WA 98107

American Physical Therapy Association
2036 Cowley Hall
La Crosse, WI 54601

National Athletic Trainers Association, Inc.
1001 East 4th Street
Greenville, NC 27834

Sports Medicine Council of Canada
333 River Road
Ottawa, Ontario, Canada K1L 8H9

Youth Development

Boys Clubs of America
7712 First Avenue
New York, NY 10017

Girl Scouts of the U.S.A.
830 3rd Avenue at 51st Street
New York, NY 10022

PART II—SPECIFIC SPORT ORGANIZATIONS

Archery

American Archery Council
618 Chalmers Street
Flint, MI 48503

National Archery Association
1750 E. Boulder Street
Colorado Springs, CO 80909

National Field Archery Association (NFAA)
RD 2, Box 514
Redlands, CA 92373

Badminton

American Badminton Association
1330 Alexandria Drive
San Diego, CA 92107

International Badminton Federation
24 Winchcombe House
Winchcombe Street, Cheltenham
Gloucestershire, England GL5 2NA

U.S. Badminton Association
P.O. Box 456
Waterford, MI 48095

Baseball

American Amateur Baseball Congress
215 East Green, Box 467
Marshall, MI 49068

American Baseball Coaches Association
605 Hamilton Drive
Champaign, IL 61820

Babe Ruth League, Inc.
P.O. Box 5000
1770 Brunswick Avenue
Trenton, NJ 08638

Baseball Canada
333 River Road
Ottawa, Ontario, Canada K1L 8H9

Casey Stengel Amateur Baseball Association, Inc.
P.O. Box 1332
Silverdale, WA 98383

Little League Baseball, Inc.
P.O. Box 3485
Williamsport, PA 17701

National Amateur Baseball Federation
2201 North Townline Road
Rose City, MI 48654

National Baseball Congress, Inc.
P.O. Box 1420
Wichita, KS 67201

Pony Baseball, Inc.
P.O. Box 225
Washington, PA 15301

U.S. Baseball Federation
4 Gregory Drive
Hamilton Square, NJ 08690

Basketball

Amateur Basketball Association of the U.S.
1750 E. Boulder Street
Colorado Springs, CO 80909

Continental Basketball Association
822 Montgomery Avenue
Narberth, PA 19072

Bicycling

Amateur Bicycling League of America
P.O. Box 699
Wall Street Station
New York, NY 10005

U.S. Cycling Federation
1750 E. Boulder Street
Colorado Springs, CO 80909

Billiards

Billiard Congress of America
717 N. Michigan Avenue
Chicago, IL 60611

Boating

American Canoe Association
4260 E. Evans Avenue
Denver, CO 80222

American Whitewater Affiliation
P.O. Box 1584
San Bruno, CA 94066

North American Yacht Racing Union
37 West 44th Street
New York, NY 10036

United States Power Squadron
50 Craig Road
Montvale, NJ 97645

Bowling

American Bowling Congress
5301 South 76th Street
Greendale, WI 53129

American Junior Bowling Congress
5301 S. 76th Street
Greendale, WI 53129

National Bowling Association
377 Park Avenue S.
7th Floor
New York, NY 10016

National Bowling Council
1919 Pennsylvania Avenue, NW
Suite 504
Washington, DC 20006

National Duck Pin Bowling
711 14th Street N.W.
Washington, DC 20005

Women's International Bowling Congress, Inc.
5301 South 76th Street
Greendale, WI 53129

Boxing

Golden Gloves Association of America
9000 Menaul, N.E.
Albuquerque, NM 87112

International Amateur Boxing Association
135 Westervelt Place
Cresskill, NJ 07626

North American Boxing Federation
708 Colorado, Suite 804
Austin, TX 78701

Casting

American Casting Association
P.O. Box 51
Nashville, TN 37202

Curling

U.S. Women's Curling Association
2792 Fairmount Boulevard
Cleveland Heights, OH 44118

Diving

U.S. Diving, Inc.
901 W. New York Street
Indianapolis, IN 46202

Fencing

Eastern Intercollegiate Fencing Association
P.O. Box 3
Centerville, MA 02632

National Intercollegiate Women's Fencing Association
235 McCosh Road
Upper Montclair, NJ 07043

United States Fencing Association, Inc.
1750 East Boulder Street
Colorado Springs, CO 80909

Football

Canadian Football League
11 King Street, W.
Suite 1800
Toronto, Ontario, Canada M5H 1A3

Pop Warner Football
1315 Walnut Street Bldg.
Suite 606
Philadelphia, PA 19107

Golf

International Golf Association
60 East 42nd Street
Room 746
New York, NY 10165

World Amateur Golf Council
Golf House
Far Hills, NJ 07931

Handball

United States Handball Association
4101 Dempster Street
Skokie, IL 60076

U.S. Team Handball Federation
1750 E. Boulder Street
Colorado Springs, CO 80909

Hiking

Intercollegiate Outing Club Association
341-G Paul Avenue
Bronx, NY 10468

National Campers and Hikers Association
7172 Transit Road
Buffalo, NY 14221

United States Orienteering Federation
P.O. Box 1081
Athens, OH 45701

Hockey

Amateur Hockey Association of the U.S.
2997 Broadmoor Valley Road
Colorado Springs, CO 80906

American Hockey League
P.O. Box 100
218 Memorial Avenue
West Springfield, MA 01089

Field Hockey Association of America, Inc.
1750 East Boulder Street
Colorado Springs, CO 80906

N.Y. Collegiate Hockey Association
Lake Hall, Room 212
State University College
Oswego, NY 13126

U.S. Field Hockey Association (Women)
1750 E. Boulder Street
Colorado Springs, CO 80909

Ice-Skating

Amateur Skating Union of the United States
1033 Shady Lane
Glen Ellyn, IL 60137

Canadian Figure Skating Association
333 River Road
Tower A, 3rd Floor
Ottawa, Ontario, Canada K1L 8H9

Ice Skating Institute of America
1000 Skokie Boulevard
Wilmette, IL 60091

United States Figure Skating Association
178 Fremont Street
Boston, MA 02111

Jogging

National Jogging Association
1910 K Street, N.W.
Washington, DC

Judo/Karate

United Karate Federation
c/o Karate Institute
315 7th Street
New York, NY 10011

United States Judo Association
4367 Bishop Road
Detroit, MI 48224

Lacrosse

The Lacrosse Foundation, Inc.
Newton H. White
Athletic Center
Baltimore, MD 21218

United States Women's Lacrosse Association
210 East Sunset Avenue
Philadelphia, PA 19118

U.S. Intercollegiate Lacrosse Association
Washington College
Chestertown, MD 21620

U.S. Women's Lacrosse Association
339 Plain Street
Mills, MA 02054

Luge

U.S. Luge Association
P.O. Box 651
Lake Placid, NY 12946

Racquet Sports

International Racquet Sports Association
132 Brookline Avenue
Boston, MA 02215

Racquetball

American Amateur Racquetball Association
815 N. Weber, Suite 203
Colorado Springs, CO 80903

American Professional Racquetball Organization
8303 E. Thomas Road
Scottsdale, AZ 85251

Riding

American Horse Shows Association
527 Madison Avenue
New York, NY 10022

National Intercollegiate Rodeo Association
P.O. Box 2088
S.H.S.V.
Huntsville, TX 77340

United States Pony Club
Pleasant Street
Dover, MA 02030

Roller Skating

Roller Skating Rink Operators Association
P.O. Box 81846
7700 "A" Street
Lincoln, NE 68501

United States of America Roller Skating Confederation
7700 "A" Street
Lincoln, NE 68510

Rowing

Canadian Amateur Rowing Association
333 River Road
Tower C, 10th Floor
Ottawa, Ontario, Canada K1L 8H9

National Rowing Foundation
P.O. Box 6030
Arlington, VA 22206

Scholastic Rowing Association of America
Saint Andrew's School
Middletown, DE 19709

U.S. Rowing Association
Four Boathouse Row
Philadelphia, PA 19130

Rugby

Eastern Rugby Union of America Incorporated
27 East State Street
Sherburne, NY 13460

U.S. Rugby Football Union Ltd.
27 East State Street
Sherburne, NY 13460

Shooting

National Rifle Association
1600 Rhode Island Ave., NW
Washington, DC 20036

National Skeet Shooting Association
2608 Inwood Rd.,
Suite 212
Dallas, TX 75235

Shuffleboard

National Shuffleboard Association
10418 NE 2nd Avenue
Miami, FL 33138

Ski

National Ski Patrol System, Inc.
2901 Sheridan Boulevard
Denver, CO 80214

Pacific Northwest Ski Association
P.O. Box 68010
Seattle, WA 98188

U.S. Ski Association
U.S. Olympic Complex
1750 E. Boulder Street
Colorado Springs, CO 80909

Soaring/Parachuting

Soaring Society of America
P.O. Box 66071
Los Angeles, CA 90066

United States Parachute Association
P.O. Box 109
Monterey, CA 93940

Soccer

American Youth Soccer Organization
5403 W. 138th Street
Hawthorne, CA 90250

Federation Internationale de Football Association
Hitzigweg 11, P.O. Box 85
Zurich, Switzerland 8030

Intercollegiate Soccer Association of America
Marist College
Poughkeepsie, NY 12601

National Intercollegiate Soccer Officials Association
131 Moffitt Boulevard
Isilip, NY 11751

National Soccer Coaches Association of America
RD #5, P.O. Box 5074
Stroudsburg, PA 18360

North American Soccer League
1133 5th Avenue, Suite 3400
New York, NY 10036

U.S. Soccer Federation
350 5th Avenue #4010
New York, NY 10118

Softball

Amateur Softball Association
2801 Northeast 50th Street
Oklahoma City, OK 73111

International Softball Congress, Inc.
6007 E. Hillcrest Circle
Anaheim Hills, CA 92807

Squash

United States Women's Squash Racquets Association
P.O. Box 962
Bryn Mawr, PA 19010

U.S. Squash Racquets Association
211 Ford Road
Bala-Cynwyd, PA 19004

Swimming

American Swimming Coaches Association
One Hall of Fame Drive
Fort Lauderdale, FL 33316

College Swimming Coaches Association of America
1000 W. Laurel
Ft. Collins, CO 80521

International Amateur Swimming Federation
2000 Financial Center
Des Moines, IA 50309

Underwater Society of America
Ambler, PA 19002

United States Swimming, Inc.
1750 E. Boulder Street
Colorado Springs, CO 80909

Tennis/Table Tennis

American Platform Tennis Association
P.O. Box 901
248 Lorraine Avenue
Upper Montclair, NJ 07043

American Tennis Association
475 Riverside Drive
Suite 439
New York, NY 10115

Association of Tennis Professionals
319 Country Club Road
Garland, TX 75040

Eastern Intercollegiate Tennis Association
P.O. Box 3
Centerville, MA 02632

Intercollegiate Tennis Coaches Association
P.O. Box 71
Princeton, NJ 08544

The Lawn Tennis Association
Palliser Road, Barons Court
W. Kensington
London, England W14 9EG

Tennis Foundation of North America
200 Castlewood Drive
North Palm Beach, FL 33408

United States Table Tennis Association
1750 E. Boulder Street
Colorado Springs, CO 80909

U.S. Paddle Tennis Association
189 Seeley Street
Brooklyn, NY 11218

U.S. Tennis Association Center for Education and Recreational Tennis
51 E. 42nd Street
New York, NY 10017

Women's Tennis Association
1604 Union Street
San Francisco, CA 94123

Track

Canadian Track and Field Association
333 River Road
Tower B, 11th Floor
Ottawa, Ontario, Canada K1L 8H9

Volleyball

National Outdoor Volleyball Association
936 Hermosa Avenue, Ste 109
Hermosa Beach, CA 90254

United States Volleyball Association
1750 E. Boulder Street
Colorado Springs, CO 80909

Waterskiing

American Water Ski Association
P.O. Box 191
Winter Haven, FL 33882

Weight Lifting

U.S. Weightlifting Federation
1750 E. Boulder Street
Colorado Springs, CO 80909

Wrestling

Canadian Amateur Wrestling
333 River Road
Ottawa, Ontario, Canada K1L 8H9

National Wrestling Coaches Association
P.O. Box 8002
Foothill Station
Salt Lake City, UT 84108

U.S. Wrestling Federation
405 W. Hall of Fame Avenue
Stillwater, OK 74074

Bibliography

Art Tuveson
University of Rhode Island

ARTICLES AND PRESENTATIONS

Aiken, B. (1984). Creative financing of sports club activities. In B.C. Vendl, L.I. Hisaka, W.M. Holsberry, G.M. Maas, & M.J. Stevenson (Eds.), *Toward an understanding of intramural-recreational sports* (pp. 358-361). Corvallis, OR: National Intramural-Recreational Sports Association.

Arnold, J. (1975). Club sports in universities and colleges. *Journal of Health, Physical Education and Recreation, 46*(8), 19-22.

Bailey, D., & Skola, S. (1980). Negotiating for club sports off-campus play spaces. In W. Holsberry, L. Marciani, & C. VosStrache (Eds.), *Intramural-recreational sports: New directions and ideas* (pp. 236-240). Corvallis, OR: National Intramural-Recreational Sports Association.

Bankhead, W. (1967). Club sports program of L.S.U. *Proceedings of the 18th Annual Conference of the National Intramural Association*, pp. 58-61.

Barnes, S.E. (1971). Sports clubs. *Journal of Health, Physical Education and Recreation, 42*(3), 23-24.

Beardsley, K. (1977). Sports club student development: Chickering's model. *28th Annual Conference Proceedings of the National Intramural-Recreational Sports Association*, 255-256.

Bennett, B.L. (1952). Students need soccer clubs. *Journal of Health, Physical Education and Recreation, 23*(8), 17.

Bishop, L. (1986). Rugby equals sportsmanship—A perspective on change. *NIRSA Journal, 10*(3), 39-40.

Braucher, W.E. (1939). Sports clubs for non-athletes in high schools. *Athletic Journal,* **20**(1), 40.

Brimi, B.A., & Ludwig, D.F. (1985). Meeting the challenge of administering a sport club program. In D.C. Bailey, E.C. Greaves, W.M. Holsberry, & J.W. Reznik (Eds.), *Management of recreational sports.* Corvallis, OR: NIRSA.

Brimi, B.A. (1986). Establishing a corrective discipline process for the sport club program. *NIRSA Journal,* **10**(3), 36-37.

Brumbach, W.B. (1973). Sport clubs—P.E.'s new partner. *Proceedings of the 77th Annual Meeting of the National College Physical Education Association for Men,* 81-87.

Bulger, H. (1968). Athletic clubs. *Proceedings of the 19th Annual Conference of the National Intramural Association,* 100-101.

Caldwell, S.Y., & Jennings, M.W. (1979). Sports club fest and 10,000 meter run. In W. Manning & C. VosStrache (Eds.), *Recreational sports programming* (pp. 126-128). Corvallis, OR: Benton Printers.

Cleave, S.L. (1984). A theoretical framework for the organization and administration of the sport club program. Part I. *Managing the sport club program from theory to practice* (pp. 1-6). Champaign, IL: Stipes.

Colgate, J. (1984). Sport clubs—Self governance and the future. In B.C. Vendl, D.C. Dutler, W.M. Holsberry, T.C. Jones, & M. Ross (Eds.), *Interpretative aspects of intramural-recreational sports* (pp. 218-225). Corvallis, OR: National Intramural-Recreational Sports Association.

Cooney, L. (1978). Sports clubs financing. In T.P. Sattler, P.J. Graham, & D.C. Bailey (Eds.), *Operational and theoretical aspects of intramural sports* (pp. 303-304). West Point, NY: Leisure Press.

Cooney, L. (1979). Sports clubs—Their place within the total intramural-recreational sports program. *Journal of Physical Education and Recreation,* **50**(3), 40-41.

Copeland, D. (1948). Intramurals through sports clubs. *Scholastic Coach,* **28**(2), 35-36.

Dabney, M.B. (1953, December). Leisure time sports clubs. *Journal of Health, Physical Education and Recreation,* **24**(10), 41-43.

Daughtrey, G. (1940). Intramural clubs. *Journal of Health, Physical Education and Recreation,* **11**(10), 613.

Denton, H. (1970). Promoting a sports club program at the University of Tennessee, Knoxville. *21st Annual Conference Proceedings of the National Intramural Association,* 94-97.

Dodson, T. (1969). Pros and cons of club sports. *Proceedings of the 72nd Annual Meeting of the National College Physical Education Association for Men*, 54-55.

Edwards, R.W. (1979). Regulations for travel and competition. *Journal of Physical Education and Recreation*, **50**(3), 48-49.

Fabian, L., & Ross, M. (1975). Administrative trends in sport club programs. *26th Annual Conference Proceedings of the National Intramural-Recreational Sports Association*, 184-185.

Fehring, W.P. (1969). Club sports. *20th Annual Conference Proceedings of the National Intramural Association*, 49-52.

Fehring, W.P. (1972). Stanford club team program. *23rd Annual Conference Proceedings of the National Intramural Association*, 68-78.

Goldammer, B., & Edmonston, C. (1984). Comparisons of university sport club programs in the Big 8, Big 10, PAC 10, Southeastern and Southwest athletic conferences. In B.C. Vendl, D.C. Dutler, W.M. Holsberry, T.C. Jones, & M. Ross (Eds.). *Interpretative aspects of intramural-recreational sports*, (pp. 225-230). Corvallis, OR: National Intramural-Recreational Sports Association.

Grambeau, R.J. (1965). Future directions and intramural sports and the NCPEAM. *Proceedings of the 68th Annual Meeting of the National College Physical Education Association for Men*, 99-102.

Grambeau, R.J. (1966). Encouraging the development of intramural sports clubs. *17th Annual Conference Proceedings of the National Intramural Association*, 115-117.

Haniford, G.W. (1958). Are sports clubs an intramural administrative responsibility? *Proceedings of the 62nd Annual Meeting of the National College Physical Education Association for Men*, 105-108.

Haniford, G.W. (1968). Sports clubs—Large colleges and universities. *9th Annual Conference Proceedings of the National Intramural Association*, 8-10.

Haniford, G.W. (1969). Pros and cons of sports clubs. *Proceedings of the 72nd Annual Meeting of the National College Physical Education Association for Men*, 49-54.

Haniford, G.W. (1972). Intramural sports clubs at Purdue University. *23rd Annual Conference Proceedings of the National Intramural Association*, 64-67.

Hass, W. (1967). Sports clubs on the campus. *Proceedings of 2nd Annual Conference of the National Association of Collegiate Directors of Athletics*, **2**, 47-52.

Heller, J., & Hills, L. (1982). Club sports: A positive approach to athletic competition. In L.S. Preo, L. Fabian, W.M. Holsberry, J.W. Reznik, &

F. Rokosz (Eds.), *Intramural-recreational sports: Its theory and practice* (pp. 132-136). Corvallis, OR: National Intramural-Recreational Sports Association.

Heller, J., & Vaughn, S. (1979). Alternative methods of sports club administration. In W. Manning & C. VosStrache (Eds.), *Recreational sports programming: Proceedings of the 30th annual conference of the National Intramural-Recreational Sports Association* (pp. 105-110). Corvallis, OR: Benton Printers.

Henry, Max (1940, November). The rifle club. *Journal of Health, Physical Education and Recreation,* **11**(9). 458.

Hess, L.A. (1971, March). Institutional committment to the financing of sports club programs. *Journal of Health, Physical Education and Recreation,* **42**, 24.

Higgins, J.R. (1948). A high school club system. *Recreation,* **42**(9), 419.

Hirt, S. (1984). Organization and administration for new club sport directors. In B.C. Vendl, D.C. Dutler, W.M. Holsberry, T.C. Jones, & M. Ross (Eds.), *Interpretative aspects of intramural-recreational sports* (pp. 212-218). Corvallis, OR: National Intramural-Recreational Sports Association.

Hirt, S., Ludwig, D.F., Capra, L., & Fletcher, M. (1984). Insurance/liability/risk management concerns in sports clubs. In B.C. Vendl, L.I. Hisaka, W.M. Holsberry, G.M. Maas, & M.J. Stevenson (Eds.), *Toward an understanding of intramural-recreational sports* (pp. 361-370). Corvallis, OR: National Intramural-Recreational Sports Association.

House, M.J., & McMurray, P.A. (1984). Sport club liability: Who is responsible? In B.C. Vendl, D.C. Dutler, W.M. Holsberry, T.C. Jones, & M. Ross (Eds.), *Interpretative aspects of intramural-recreational sports* (pp. 230-234). Corvallis, OR: National Intramural-Recreational Sports Association.

Hyatt, R.W. (1976). Sports clubs: Organization and administration. In J.A. Peterson (Ed.), *Intramural administration: Theory and practice* (pp. 226-244). Englewood Cliffs, NJ: Prentice-Hall.

Jamerson, R.E. (1969). Pros and cons of sports clubs. *Proceedings of the 72nd Annual Meeting of the National College Physical Association for Men,* 41-49.

Jeter, J. (1977). A possible solution to NCAA recognition of sports clubs. *28th Annual Conference Proceedings of the National Intramural-Recreational Sports Association,* 252-254.

Jeter, J.M. (1979). Extramural sports clubs and varsity athletics. *Journal of Physical Education and Recreation,* **50**(3), 42-43.

Johnson, W.P. (1971). The club approach to intercollegiate athletics in a new community college. *Journal of Health, Physical Education and Recreation, 42*(24), 25.

Junker, D.F., Anderson, B.D., & Mueller, D.E. (1975). Sport club development—70's community involvement. *26th Annual Conference Proceedings of the National Intramural-Recreational Sports Association,* 144-147.

Loveless, J.C., & Post, E.G. (1941). The college outing club. *Recreation, 44*(9), 558.

Maas, G.M. (1979, March). The sports club council—A vital administrative tool. *Journal of Physical Education and Recreation, 50*(3), 45.

Marshall, S. (1968). Athletic directors' survey. *National Association of Collegiate Directors of Athletic Quarterly, 3*(1, Pt. 2).

Mason, D. (1978). Sports club program. In T.P. Sattler, P.J. Graham, & D.C. Bailey (Eds.), *Operational and theoretical aspects of intramural sports* (pp. 302-303). West Point, NY: Leisure Press.

Matthews, D.O. (1965). Sports club organization. *Scholastic Coach, 5*(50), 72-74.

Matthews, D.O. (1969). The new look in university and college intramurals. *Proceedings of the 73rd Annual Meeting of the National College Physical Education Association for Men,* 6-10.

Matthews, D.O. (1978). Organizing sports clubs for secondary schools. *NIRSA Journal, 3*(1), 38-41.

Matthews, D.O. (1979). The responsibility of colleges for administering a sports club program. *NIRSA Journal, 3*(2), 24-35.

McCoy, E.B. (1967). Sports clubs on campus. *2nd Annual Proceedings of the National Association of Collegiate Directors of Athletics, 2,* 52-62.

McDonough, T.E. (1937). The athletic club as the medium for intramural competition. *Journal of Health and Physical Education, 8*(6), 380.

McNeeley, P.R., & Capra, L. (1983). Fund raising—Getting down to the nitty gritty. In B.G. Lamke, M.P. Holmes, W.M. Holsberry, & C. Meyers (Eds.), *Process and concepts in recreational sports* (pp. 213-219). Corvallis, OR: National Intramural-Recreational Sports Association.

Mendelsohn, E.J. (1956). Recent trends and development of extramural activities in colleges and universities. *Proceedings of the 59th Annual Meeting of the National College Physical Education Association for Men,* 155-159.

Mull, R.F. (1979). Toward a club sport foundation. In W. Manning & C. VosStrache (Eds.), *Recreational sports programming: Proceedings of the 30th annual conference of the National Intramural-Recreational Sports Association* (pp. 112-116). Corvallis, OR: Benton Printers.

Omann, G. (1978). Cost analysis of sports clubs, 1974-77. In T.P. Sattler, P.J. Graham, & D.C. Bailey (Eds.), *Operational and theoretical aspects of intramural sports*, (pp. 317-320). West Point, NY: Leisure Press.

Palmateer, D. (1978, February). Survey showing current practices in club sports funding. *NIRSA Journal*, 2(2), 6-9.

Palmateer, D.(1979, March). The dollars and sense approach to sport club funding. *Journal of Physical Education and Recreation*, 50(3), 46-67.

Parberry, C. (1972). Sports clubs at the University of Idaho. *24th Annual Conference Proceedings of the National Intramural Association*, 67-68.

Pariseau, J. (1972). Sports clubs of the student, for the student. *7th Annual Proceedings of the Association of Collegiate Directors of Athletics*, 58-67.

Parsons, N.C. (1975). Sport clubs—You gotta believe. *26th Annual Conference Proceedings of the National Intramural-Recreational Sports Association*, 162-165.

Parsons, N.C. (1979). Legal liability and sports clubs. In W. Manning & C. VosStrache (Eds.), *Recreational sports programming: Proceedings of the 30th annual conference of the National Intramural-Recreational Sports Association (pp. 120-126).*

Phelps, D.E. (1970). Current practices and recommended guidelines for the administration of sports clubs in selected four-year midwest colleges and universities. *21st Annual Conference Proceedings of the National Intramural Association*, 32-36.

Preo, L.S. (1977). *28th Annual Conference Proceedings of the National Intramural-Recreational Sports Association*, 54-56.

Radde, G.I. (1977). A student's perception of sports club administration and responsibility at the University of Minnesota. *28th Annual Conference Proceedings of the National Intramural-Recreational Sports Association*, 260-261.

Rankin, J.S., & Fraki, A.N. (1982). Current problems in liability in campus recreation, intramurals and sport clubs. In L.S. Preo, L. Fabian, W.M. Holsberry, J.W. Reznik, & F. Rokosz, (Eds.). *Intramural-recreational sports: Its theory and practice* (pp. 24-35). Corvallis, OR: National Intramural-Recreational Sports Association.

Schechter, S. (1981). Sports clubs: An evolution. *NIRSA Journal*, 5(2), 52-55.

Skola, S.A. (1982). Athletic training and coaching: A seminar for club sports. In L.S. Preo, L. Fabian, W.M. Holsberry, J.W. Reznik, & F. Rokosz (Eds.), *Intramural-recreational sports: Its theory and practice*. Corvallis, OR: National Intramural-Recreational Sports Association.

Sliger, I.T. (1970, February). An extensive sports club program. *Journal of Health, Physical Education and Recreation,* **41**(2), 39-40.

Sliger, I.T. (1978). Sports club survey. (Unpublished Internal Report) University of Tennessee, Knoxville.

Steilberg, P. (1970). A future look at intramural and recreation programs at colleges and universities in the U.S. *Proceedings of the 74th Annual Meeting of the National College Physical Education Association for Men,* 263-264.

Stevenson, M. (1971). The impact of sports club growth on intramural programs. *22nd Annual Conference Proceedings of the National Intramural Association,* 35-39.

Stewart, S.J. (1978). Sports clubs and financing. In T.P. Sattler, P.J. Graham, & D.C. Bailey (Eds.), *Operational and theoretical aspects of intramural sports,* (pp. 303-305). West Point, NY: Leisure Press.

Stewart, S.L. (1982). An administrative support system for club sports. In L.S. Preo, L. Fabian, W. Holsberry, J.W. Reznik, & F. Rokasz (Eds.), *Intramural-recreational sports: Its theory and practice* (pp. 136-141). Corvallis, OR: National Intramural-Recreational Sports Association.

Stratton, S. (1977). A student's development through sports clubs. *28th Annual Conference Proceedings of the National Intramural-Recreational Sports Association,* 258-260.

Stratton-Rusch, S. (1978). Sports clubs officer personal development inventory. In T.P. Sattler, P.J. Graham, & D.C. Bailey (Eds.), *Operational and theoretical aspects of intramural sports* (pp. 306-316). West Point, NY: Leisure Press.

Taylor, D.H. (1977). Athletic training curriculum at West Virginia University and its application to intramural and club sports. *28th Annual Proceedings of the National Intramural-Recreational Sports Association,* 191-192.

Teague, J. (1979). Policies and procedures for effective sports club administration. In W. Manning & C. VosStrache (Eds.), *Recreational Sports Programming: Proceedings of the 30th annual conference of the National Intramural-Recreational Sports Association* (pp. 117-120). Corvallis, OR: Benton Printers.

Teague, J. (1979). The sports club president and advisor. *Journal of Physical Education and Recreation,* **50**(3), 44.

Thornton, S., & Imdieke, M. (1978). Habilis, a new, innovative development in sports clubs at the University of Minnesota. In T.P. Sattler, P.J. Graham, & D.C. Bailey (Eds.), *Operational and theoretical aspects of intramural sports* (pp. 324-327). West Point, NY: Leisure Press.

Tonsager, G. (1977). The development of the individual through sports clubs. *28th Annual Conference Proceedings of the National Intramural-Recreational Sports Association,* 256-258.

Tuveson, A. (1980, February). Club sports' fund raising alternatives. *NIRSA Journal,* 4(2), 18-20.

Williamson, W.E. (1979). Financing sports clubs. In S. Manning & C. VosStrache (Eds.), *Recreational sports programming: Proceedings of the 30th annual conference of the National Intramural-Recreational Sports Association* (pp. 110-112). Corvallis: Benton Printers.

Zygadlo, R. (1974). The best solicitors of public support for sports clubs. *25th Annual Conference Proceedings of the National Intramural Association,* 44-45.

UNPUBLISHED MASTER'S THESES AND DOCTORAL DISSERTATIONS

Becker, R.E. (1965). *A survey of men's sports clubs in selected colleges and universities in the United States.* Unpublished master's thesis, University of Washington, Seattle.

Grambeau, R.J. (1959). *A survey of the administration of intramural sports programs for men in selected colleges and universities in North and South America.* Unpublished doctoral dissertation, University of Michigan, Ann Arbor.

Johnson, H. (1974). *Recommended procedures for the administration of men's club sports programs at selected American colleges and universities.* Unpublished doctoral dissertation, New York University, New York.

Phelps, D.E. (1970). *Current practices and recommended guidelines for the administration of sports clubs in selected four-year midwest colleges and univer-sites.* Unpublished doctoral dissertation, Indiana University, Bloomington.

Vinson, M.M. (1975). *A comparison of extramural sports programs in four-year institutions in the state of Utah.* Unpublished master's thesis, Brigham Young University, Salt Lake City.

BOOKS

American Association for Health, Physical Education, and Recreation. (1968). *Campus recreation.* Washington, DC: National Education Association.

Bucher, C.A. (1983). *Administration of physical education & athletic programs* (8th ed.). St. Louis: C.V. Mosby.

Daughtrey, G., & Woods, J.E. (1977). *Physical education and intramural programs: Organization and administration.* St. Louis: C.V. Mosby.

Fisher, C.E., Boucher, R., Holsberry, W.M., & Varner, H.S. (1986). *Growth and development in recreational sports.* Corvallis, OR: NIRSA.

Hyatt, R.W. (1977). *Intramural sports: Organization and administration.* St. Louis: C.V. Mosby.

Peterson, J.A. (1976). *Intramural administration: Theory and practice.* Englewood Cliffs, NJ: Prentice-Hall.

Kleindienst, V.K., & Weston, A. (1968). *Intramural and recreation programs for schools and colleges.* New York: Meridith Publishing.

Leavitt, N.H., & Price, H.D. (1950). *Intramural and recreational sports for high school and colleges.* New York: Ronald Press.

Manning, W., & VosStrache, C. (Eds.). (1979). *Recreational sports programming: Proceedings of the 30th annual conference of the National Intramural-Recreational Sports Association.* Corvallis, OR: Benton Printers.

Means, L.E. (1963). *Intramurals: Their organization and administration.* Englewood Cliffs, NJ: Prentice-Hall.

Mitchell, E.D. (1939). *Intramural sports.* New York: A.S. Barnes.

Mueller, C.E. (1971). *Intramurals: Programming and administration.* New York: Ronald Press.

Mueller, C.E., & Mitchell, E.D. (1960). *Intramural sports.* New York: Ronald Press.

Mueller, C.E., & Reznik, J.W. (1979). *Intramural-recreational sports* (5th ed.). New York: John Wiley.

Preo, L.S., Fabian, L., Holsberry, W.M., Reznik, J.W., & Rokosz, F. (Eds.). (1982). *Intramural-recreational sports: Its theory and practice.* Corvallis, OR: National Intramural-Recreational Sports Association.

Resick, M.C., & Erickson, C.E. (1975). *Intercollegiate and interscholastic athletics for men and women.* Reading, MA: Addison-Wesley.

Sattler, T.P., Graham, P.J., & Bailey, D.C. (Eds.). (1978). *Operational and theoretical aspects of intramural sports.* West Point, NY: Leisure Press.

Vendl, B.C., Dutler, D.C., Holsberry, W.M., Jones, T.C., Ross, M. (Eds.). (1984). *Interpretative aspects of intramural-recreational sports.* Corvallis, OR: National Intramural-Recreational Sports Association.

Vendl, B.C., Hisaka, L.I., Holsberry, W.M., Maas, G.M., & Stevenson, M.J. (Eds.). (1984). *Toward an understanding of intramural-recreational sports.* Corvallis, OR: National Intramural-Recreational Sports Association.